Jake Wallis Simons is an award-winning British journalist and novelist. Formerly a foreign correspondent who has worked for the BBC and national newspapers, he is now Editor of the *Jewish Chronicle*, where he has become known for publishing world exclusives, often about Iran and the Mossad. In addition, he is a writer for the *Spectator*, a commentator for Sky News and a broadcaster for BBC Radio 4 and the World Service.

Praise for *Israelophobia*:

'Timely and important . . . An exhaustive and damning study'

Telegraph, Book of the Year

'This book is particularly timely . . . makes a convincing exposé of the convenient line that attacks on Israel'

Evening Standard

'There never was a more timely publication than *Israelophobia* by Jake Wallis Simons'

Rod Liddle

'This is an important and necessary book by a superb and subtle writer. There's no one more qualified to write it than Jake Wallis Simons, both as ground-breaking Middle East security correspondent and Editor of the *Jewish Chronicle*. It analyses the often prejudiced coverage and intense scrutiny of Israel that so often veers into obsession and outright demonisation; and traces its origins from Medieval European and Stalinist antisemitism to the present day. It discusses why this nation is judged so differently from others in a supposedly rational and progressive era. A companion in some ways to David Baddiel's *Jews Don't Count*, it is a book that fascinatingly analyses the dark sides of our world today – political, national, cultural and digital – and exposes uncomfortable truths'

Simon Sebag Montefiore

'"I can't be antisemitic: I have nothing against Jews individually, I only hate them by the country." Such is the delusion that Jake Wallis Simons sets out to discredit in this excellent and fearless book, dismantling its mendacities with a scholarly and logical thoroughness that makes you wonder if there will ever be an Israelophobe left standing again. Buy copies to distribute to your kindergarten groups and universities, anyway, just in case. And then buy another copy for yourself. It does the heart good to see one of the greatest expressions of collective animus exposed for the sanctimonious posturing it is. *Israelophobia* is a book we all need'

Howard Jacobson

'A profoundly powerful polemic'

Rob Rinder

Israelophobia

The Newest Version of the Oldest Hatred and What To Do About It

JAKE WALLIS SIMONS

CONSTABLE

CONSTABLE

First published in Great Britain in 2023 by Constable
This paperback edition published in 2024 by Constable

3 5 7 9 10 8 6 4 2

Image credits: p72 akg-images/De Agostini Picture Library; p74 Chronicle/Alamy Stock Photo; p137 Keystone/Getty Images; p169 akg-images/Fototeca Gilardi

A CIP catalogue record for this book
is available from the British Library.

ISBN: 978-1-40871-928-2

Typeset in Electra by Hewer Text UK Ltd, Edinburgh
Printed and bound in Great Britain by Clays Ltd, Elcograf, S.p.A.

Papers used by Constable are from well-managed forests and other responsible sources.

FSC
www.fsc.org
MIX
Paper | Supporting responsible forestry
FSC® C104740

Constable
An imprint of
Little, Brown Book Group
Carmelite House
50 Victoria Embankment
London EC4Y 0DZ

The authorised representative
in the EEA is
Hachette Ireland
8 Castlecourt Centre
Dublin 15, D15 XTP3, Ireland
(email: info@hbgi.ie)

An Hachette UK Company

www.hachette.co.uk

www.littlebrown.co.uk

For Roxanna and our children

'We are a people as all other peoples; we do not have any intentions to be better than the rest. As one of the first conditions for equality we demand the right to have our own villains, exactly as other people have them.' *Ze'ev Jabotinsky, 1911*

'Be disappointed, as we are all to a degree disappointed, that the great, adventurous ambitions of Zionism, to avert imminent catastrophe, to rejuvenate a too long confused and slumbering faith, to chart a course between aggressive assimilation and timorous isolationism, to live in peace with neighbours, have not yet, in all instances, achieved their goals. But don't allow the disappointments of now to distort the ambitions of then. Just because iniquity appears sometimes to be its fruit does not mean that Zionism was iniquitous in its planting. It is in the tragic nature of dreams to evaporate. For which we weep. The grander the vanished dream, the more copious our tears should be. And to those who will not weep, who would rather march, protest and boycott, I say: You are among those who wanted to see the dream blighted in the first place.' *Howard Jacobson*

Contents

FOREWORD: AFTER 7 OCTOBER xi

1 THE NEWEST HATRED 1
2 WHAT IS ISRAELOPHOBIA? 21
3 DEMONISATION 27
4 WEAPONISATION 77
5 FALSIFICATION 131
6 THE EIGHT GIVEAWAYS AND THE FIVE PRESSURE POINTS 183

ACKNOWLEDGEMENTS 193
NOTES 195

Foreword: After 7 October

I TOLD YOU SO

If 'I told you so' moments commonly constitute some small triumph, the one delivered by October 2023 brought only despair and dread. This book was published on 7 September, precisely a month before Israel's southern defences collapsed and its enemies went on a rampage of murder, rape and mutilation that was unparalleled since the Holocaust. That day and the months that followed provided a relentless stream of evidence for the analysis contained within these pages. How I wished that I had been wrong.

Since 7 October, Jews have been forced to acknowledge that the lessons of history which we hoped had been learnt had not been learnt at all. They had only disrupted the traditional unfolding of the hatred. It wasn't just the Nazi years that were revived on 7 October. In Baghdad in 1941, bodies were mutilated; in Kishinev in 1903, babies were torn to pieces by the mob; in 1834, in the mystical city of Safed in northern Palestine, women were stripped and raped; in the Iberian Peninsula in 1391, Jews were butchered in their thousands; in York in 1290, Jews were burned alive in

Clifford's Tower. It most of these cases, the slow progress of everyday bigotry had climaxed in an orgy of violence. In 2023, however, an orgy of violence gave way to the emergence of everyday bigotry.

Around the world, many Jews now face graffiti on their schools, homes and places of worship – a slogan about Gaza was scrawled outside my house – and weekly marches calling for their eradication. On a cultural level, the spread of the new antisemitism has continued apace, beginning in the elite institutions and among the youth and seeping outwards from there, in a mechanism foretold in this book. A recent poll in the United States found that two-thirds of young people saw Jews as 'oppressors' and thought they should be treated as such.[1] And what do we do about oppressors? As I wrote in the pages that follow, the core mechanism of antisemitism is that demonisation demands destruction. If the Jews of the Nazi imagination were malign by their very nature, it was natural to endorse the harsh but urgent project of exterminating them. If the Jews of Medieval Europe had killed Christ, it was natural to drive them out, murder them or convert them under torture. Likewise, if the Jews are unable to help themselves from indulging their natural taste for genocide, ethnic cleansing, white supremacy, colonialism, occupation, apartheid and revelling in the blood of children – if they are repeating what the Nazis did to them – they forfeit their right to a homeland. They forfeit their right to go about their lives free from bullying. They forfeit their right to exist.

That Israelophobia is the newest face of the oldest hatred can no longer be reasonably doubted. After 7 October, those who are most concerned with virtue have been the most abominable, but as this book makes clear, the capacity of antisemitism to masquerade as a virtue has always been one of its hallmarks. None of the perpetrators of the past considered that they were in the wrong. They believed they were erasing moral corruption for the good of the world. Similarly, it does not seem likely that the Hamas savages, who filmed their crimes on GoPros and exulted to their parents on the phones of their victims, felt any guilt. I suppose it is possible that the western liberals who make excuses for the atrocities; who hold the 'occupation' responsible, despite Israel's unilateral withdrawal from Gaza in 2005; who refuse to assimilate Hamas's obvious gameplan – to massacre Jews then hide behind babies while beckoning the television cameras – into their reckoning that laid the blame at the door of the Jews; who harbour selective outrage when it comes to rape, experienced the occasional prick of shame in their hearts, as did many ordinary Germans. But perhaps I'm wrong. Perhaps they remain so convinced of the supposed virtue of their opposition to Israel that their moral degradation, seen so clearly by the rest of us, remains obscure to them. Either way, if they have felt the pang of conscience at all, it has evidently been easily repressed.

The very people who build their identities around #MeToo and #believewomen and #silenceisviolence, who hyperventilate at the sin of misgendering, who can detect a microaggression at twenty paces, who require trigger warnings for performances of Romeo and Juliet, who see racism everywhere, have suddenly developed a stomach for such things, have suddenly been able to cite 'the context'. As Howard Jacobson put it: 'It would seem that a massacre is not small enough to be a worry.[2]

Rather than unite behind a beleaguered democracy on the front line in the war on jihadism, these people have blamed the Jews for their own massacre, warning them that to mount a defence against such unvarnished evil – as other democracies have done against Islamic State or the Third Reich – would make them guilty of crimes against humanity. When is collateral damage not collateral damage? When it's the Jews doing the killing. While other democracies wage war, the Jews wage genocide. In London, New York and elsewhere, mobs took to the street began even before Israeli jets were in the skies. What were these people demonstrating against? The Israelis had done nothing but get themselves slaughtered. That first day lifted the mask. Appallingly, the activists were demonstrating *for* something: Jewish destruction.

As the months went by and demands for the genocide of Jews rang out weekly across our cities, it became clear that at the core of the protests were those who glorified an act of depravity refashioned as anti-colonial resistance. (When Hamas mutilated corpses, butchered babies and toyed with severed heads, it was a reaction to Jewish oppression. When they committed bestial sexual violence, they had been pushed to it by imperialism. Anyway, who could guarantee that the footage had not been fabricated?) Thousands of apparently well-meaning progressive were prepared to turn a blind eye to blood-curdling chants and placards simply because their political identities were at stake. Tens of thousands saw Gazans suffering on television, wanted an end to the killing and thought it likely that the Jews were to blame. What's that term again? Ah, yes. Unconscious bias.

Yes, 7 October has made it impossible to deny the dominance of Israelophobia on the political left, the anatomisation of which forms a significant part of this book. In November, I received a message from an old university friend with whom I had lost touch almost ten years before. 'I'm sorry for de-friending you on Facebook,' she wrote. 'When you went to work for right wing media, I thought you'd gone off the rails. I'm eating my words now. The left – which is where I've always positioned myself – has become extremist, not to mention, apparently, bloodthirsty. I basically bowed out a year or so ago on the issue of women's and children's rights vs. the trans mob but outright support for the brutal annihilation of Israel is a new fucking low. Feeling extremely isolated right now.' She was speaking for many. At the *Jewish Chronicle*, the newspaper I edit, we had an idea to run a feature about the non-Jewish voices who had stuck up for Israel in the media. We could not think of any on the left.

The most eye-popping example of progressive Israelophobia came in December when the principals of America's three most esteemed universities, Harvard, UPenn and MIT, were unable to condemn calls for the genocide of Jews without reaching for 'the context'. The shame they brought upon their institutions was laid bare by an AI-generated video in which the question was exchanged for one about demands for the genocide of black, gay or Muslim people. What context could there be for demanding the extermination of Africans? What context for the murder of trans people? There could be no clearer illustration of the double standards of antisemitism. The fact that progressives have become gripped by the oldest bigotry, cloaked in its newest guise of Israelophobia, can no longer be sensibly denied.

The three academics were not alone in excusing the inexcusable by citing 'the context'. António Guterres, the Secretary-General of the United Nations, did the same, arguing that the beheading of babies was 'did not happen in a vacuum', which many felt was a justification by implication with a nudge and a wink. In this way, he drew lurid attention to the Israelophobia that has long dominated at the UN, another topic explored in this book. On 8 October, before the blood was dry in southern Israel, the Security Council met but was unable to reach a consensus condemning Hamas's 'heinous terrorist attacks', so no statement was released. Despite further sessions, more than two weeks later, there had still been no condemnation; it wasn't until 15 November that a resolution was finally adopted, and this called for 'urgent and extended humanitarian pauses' and the release of hostages, but did not mention the 7 October atrocities.

Similarly, it took eight weeks of silence for UN Women, the organisation's women's rights body, to condemn Hamas's sexual hyper-violence, and even then, its statement led with 'regret' over hostilities in Gaza. Of course, resolutions demanding a ceasefire – code for calling upon Jews to lay down their weapons until they are exterminated – have been rigorously pursued. To readers of *Israelophobia*, none of this would have been surprising. As the 1960s Israeli diplomat Abba Eban once remarked: 'If Algeria introduced a resolution declaring that the Earth was flat and that Israel had flattened it, it would pass by a vote of 164 to 13, with 26 abstentions.'[3]

As the columnist Bret Stephens wrote in the *New York Times* a month after the atrocities, for Jews, every day is now 8 October.[4] It can be hard to recall the world of 6 October with any vividness: it feels like a million years ago. Looking back at the opening of my book, which was written at the end of that old period, it is revealing in new ways. The first chapter describes the rallies that took place in London in 2021, when 256 Palestinians lost their lives in a clash between Hamas and Israel. We have since seen the same scenes on steroids. How measures of trauma have changed, and how quickly! Nonetheless, the 2021 example retains its power; if 180,000 people turned out to protest Israel in Hyde Park after such a relatively small number of deaths, especially while far bigger wars raged in Syria and Yemen, that proved my point even more conclusively. On the other hand, in October 2023, the situation was even more clear-cut. Hamas targeted Israelis living firmly within their internationally recognised borders. Many of them were peace activists who learned Arabic so that they could ferry their ailing Gazan neighbours to hospital in Israel, or who had planned to fly kites for peace on the afternoon of the day they were killed. The anti-Israel rallies around the world precipitated by these murders could not be plausibly ascribed to anything other than Israelophobia.

Further in this book, I quote George Orwell: 'one of the marks of antisemitism is an ability to believe stories that could not possibly be true'.[5] Once again, this rule has been confirmed with depressing conclusiveness since the October atrocities, which have also demonstrated that the opposite can be the case. Disturbingly, the viral strain of Holocaust denial has found a new expression in burgeoning Hamas massacre denial. The Palestinian killers filmed themselves committing their crimes and shared the footage wantonly. How much more evidence do you need? But denial is never about the evidence. It is about piling humiliation upon the Jews by casting doubt on their suffering. The antisemite, an old saying goes, accuses a Jew of theft merely for the pleasure of seeing him turn out his pockets.

Other more subtle lies are now commonplace. Take the notion that Gaza was an 'open-air prison camp', used so often to excuse the Hamas savagery. How could people seriously believe that Gaza had been a sealed territory for decades while also criticising Israel for no longer providing extra water, food and fuel into the Strip? How could they at once demand that Israel resume deliveries of lorryloads of aid and condemn the Jewish state for keeping Gazans in a state of starvation for years?

Let us look at the facts. Israel withdrew from Gaza unilaterally in 2005, leaving the Palestinians the keys to their kibbutzim (which were then destroyed in Israelophobic rage). Even after Hamas took over the Strip and used all its resources for the construction of terror infrastructure, Israel continued to provide humanitarian goods and services. There was a military blockade, of course, and the reason for that was made grimly clear in October. But Israel allowed tens of thousands of Gazans to enter its territory daily to work, in the belief that the influx of money into the failing economy of the Strip would create a measure of stability and reduce the chances of aggression. Among those Palestinians who took advantage of

Israeli generosity were spies gathering intelligence that was used on 7 October. One of the most sobering stories to have emerged was of two photographers, one Israeli and the other Gazan, who put on joint exhibitions. It later emerged that the Palestinian had used his counterpart's pictures of her home to create a map of her kibbutz that was used by the Hamas butchers. We know now that whatever the Jewish state does will not release it from the grip of the hate mob. It could kill zero civilians and still be criticised (indeed, as I mention on page seven, this happened in Jenin in July 2023).

Menachem Begin, the founder of Likud and a former prime minister of Israel, said: 'I am not a Jew with trembling knees. I am a proud Jew with 3,700 years of civilised history. Nobody came to our aid when we were dying in the gas chambers and ovens. Nobody came to our aid when we were striving to create our country. We paid for it. We fought for it. We died for it. We will stand by our principles. We will defend them. And, when necessary, we will die for them again.'[6] This may be true for Israelis. But the appetite for the Jews is never sated by swallowing the Jews. The mobs marching on the streets seek the demise of the Jewish people simply as the most prominent expressions of western liberal values. They have attacked the monuments and flags of Britain, the United States and other democracies while also calling for the deaths of Jews. In the weeks after the attacks, many Israelis said to me: 'We will get through this. But how are *you*?' This is our problem. The wave of subversion that is rising from within democratic societies is one that threatens to subsume us all in time. That is why Israelophobia matters. If we are to return any measure of sanity to the debate, and if we are to save our societies from themselves, the arguments contained in this book are urgent.

JWS

Chapter One

THE NEWEST HATRED

We want their blood

'This is the Nike anti-Jewish edition,' jokes the young man, showing off the miniature Israeli flags that he has attached to his trainers. It is a Sunday afternoon in central London and a rowdy demonstration is being held outside the Israeli embassy to protest the conflict with Hamas. The previous day saw one of the largest pro-Palestinian rallies in British history, with 180,000 people crowding Hyde Park. This smaller gathering was drummed up to oppose a pro-Israel group. A few streets away from the man with the antisemitic trainers, a gang prowls the backstreets. 'We'll find some Jews here,' one shouts. 'We want the Zionists. We want their blood.' Two police officers nearby hear him but do nothing. Meanwhile, back in the heart of the mob, a bearded firebrand roars into a megaphone against a backdrop of young men, many of whom wear black masks, holding Palestinian flags. 'The difference between us and them is that for them, they think life begins,' he bellows towards the pro-Israel crowd. 'For us, we believe that death begins. We believe that life begins at death. We don't care about death. We love death.'[1]

These scenes took place in May 2021, but they remain lodged in the memory of many British Jews. At the time, Israel was locked in combat with Gazan terrorists, who had fired more than four thousand rockets at Tel Aviv, Jerusalem and other population centres in Israel, and wherever you looked, hatred was boiling over. The day before, on the Jewish Sabbath, the man who boasted of his love of death – a former trainee history teacher called Mohammed Hijab – had filmed himself in the heart of London's Jewish community, harassing Orthodox men by asking whether they had 'learned from the Holocaust' in front of a mobile billboard showing pictures of Jews in concentration camps. The previous week, a convoy of cars flying Palestinian flags had rolled through north London, with men leaning out of the windows and yelling through megaphones: 'Fuck the Jews; rape their daughters.' The husband of the Israeli ambassador and their three small daughters had been surrounded but had managed to drive away unscathed.

Looking back at events like these, many Jews are shocked by how little they are shocked. Jewish schools, synagogues and community centres are forced to live with a level of security that is required by no other minority. According to Home Office figures, despite comprising just 0.5 per cent of the population, British Jews face nearly a quarter of all hate crimes[2] and are five times more likely to be targeted than other faith groups.[3] Fifty-five per cent say they have suffered racism, compared to 50 per cent of black Caribbeans and 30 per cent of black Africans, the Evidence for Equality National

Survey reported.[4] Antisemitic incidents are soaring across the western world, rising by 36 per cent in 2022 to hit an all-time high in the United States alone.[5] In France, more than 60 per cent of religious abuse is directed at Jews,[6] and in Germany, anti-Jewish hate crime rose from 1,374 incidents in 2012 to 2,639 in 2022.[7] The prejudice that predominates today is different to the antisemitism of old, however. Around the globe, most anti-Jewish bigotry now focuses not on their religion or race, but their homeland.

As editor of the world's oldest Jewish newspaper, the *Jewish Chronicle* – and before that a foreign correspondent, who also reported extensively on antisemitism in Jeremy Corbyn's Labour Party – I have long been aware of the hatred that squats at the dark heart of the anti-Israel movement. Despite being the Middle East's only liberal democracy, where gay people, women and minorities live more freely than anywhere else in the region, Israel is often smeared as the world's most oppressive regime; those who oppose it in the most fanatical and chauvinistic terms, even with kitchen knives, homemade guns and suicide bombs, are portrayed as standing up to tyranny. In the liberal west, the pro-Palestinian cause is embraced as a totem of identity politics, equated with resistance to apartheid South Africa, colonialism and white supremacy. Israeli products are boycotted; Israeli businesses are vandalised; Israeli speakers are hounded out of universities; and all is presented as if the demons are on the side of the angels.

The public is encouraged to believe that hating the Jewish state is an entirely different matter from hating Jews. But it doesn't take long for the mask to slip. Take the mass demonstrations of May 2021, which were sparked by Israeli military action taken in response to Hamas's rockets. By the time hostilities had abated, 256 Palestinians, most of them terrorists, and fourteen Israeli civilians lay dead (further Israeli casualties were prevented by the Iron Dome missile defence system, which intercepted and destroyed more than 1,200 rockets before they could land on homes and offices).[8] Why did the protesters choose to highlight this particular conflict so vehemently? That year, United Nations (UN) records showed[9] that numerous wars, injustices, human rights abuses and atrocities were taking place all over the world, including on Israel's doorstep. Syria had reached a grim milestone of ten years of war, with more than half-a-million lives lost. Yemen, named as the location of the world's most severe humanitarian crisis, was facing the highest levels of acute malnutrition since the conflict began, with over half the population experiencing severe food shortages, and ten thousand children killed or maimed since the start of the fighting.

Violence was raging in Tigray, Ethiopia, placing 350,000 people at risk of famine. A coup in Myanmar was pushing twenty-five million people, nearly half the population, into poverty. UN peacekeepers were being killed in Mali, where 400,000 people fled their homes due to violence and nearly five million were reliant on humanitarian aid. Yet it was the Israel conflict, with its 270 dead, that provoked such large and bitter demonstrations around the world. Why? There are many possible explanations. But clues may lie in the death worshipper outside the embassy, the Zionist blood prowlers in the backstreets and the megaphone men who wished to rape Jewish daughters.

Israel is far from perfect. In addition to covering the region extensively both at the *Jewish Chronicle* and in my previous jobs at the *Daily Mail*, the *Sunday Telegraph* and elsewhere, I've spent years reporting from all over the world, from Caracas to Colombo, from St Helene to Harare, from the Bataclan to the badlands of Maiduguri. I've been teargassed more than once on the West Bank. I have seen enough countries in various states of crisis – to borrow from Tolstoy – to know that every unhappy nation is unhappy in its own way. Since Benjamin Netanyahu became prime minister in 2022 at the head of a coalition that included several extremists, Israel's flaws have become particularly visible, with rallies across the land amid a crisis of its democratic system. Yet every country is also admirable in its own way. When measured in terms of corruption, human rights, democracy, liberty and so on, the Jewish state tends to rank mid-table or higher. In the final analysis, it is just another country, with its own qualities and its own sins. Why is it not judged by the standards applied to all other nations? Why is it pilloried, boycotted, undermined, vilified and abused? And how to separate reasonable criticism from hatred?

Here's the problem

Antisemitism has become one of the most politicised and explosive topics of our times. In recent years, it has come to dominate news cycles, column inches, culture wars and kitchen table conversations, and has been feverishly debated by politicians. It has created new alliances and new enemies, spawning waves of activists on all sides of the argument and conspiracy theories in dark corners of the internet. There have been rallies; there have been debates; there have been lawsuits; there have been scandals. There have been viral videos and Twitter storms. It has broken friendships, divided generations and crashed political movements. But as society has been trying to get a grip on the phenomenon, it has been evolving out of reach.

The old antisemitism was a known quantity. It was cartoons of Jews with hook noses and bags of money. It was Fagin and *The Merchant of Venice*. In particular, it was dead Jews: the Spanish Inquisition, the pogroms of eastern Europe and the Holocaust. Israel, however, is another matter. It does not conform to our familiar mental image of Jews queuing for the gas chambers. It fights back. Its fighter jets swoop regularly over Auschwitz, piloted by the children of Holocaust survivors. Its citizens are physically strong, patriotic and assertive, a long way from self-hating Woody Allen stereotypes. With social media awash with images of bombs falling on Palestinian children and bulldozers demolishing Palestinian homes, people whisper behind their hands that the Jewish state has become everything it once stood against. As the American writer Dara Horn memorably put it: 'People love dead Jews. Living Jews, not so much.'[10]

As you might expect from a post-colonial democracy in a turbulent and hostile region, Israel doesn't get everything right. But the level of opprobrium it receives goes way beyond its faults. It is slandered online, singled out for hatred at the UN, subjected to international boycott, and attacked in every conceivable way, from digital propaganda to guerrilla poster campaigns to university campus rallies. The hostility heaped on the Middle East's only democratic state, and the only Jewish country on Earth, dwarfs that directed at the cruellest autocracies. It is held to standards expected of no other state. It is smeared in the most lurid terms, accused of everything from ethnic cleansing to white supremacy, colonialism, infanticide and mass murder. When it takes surgical military action to defend itself from terrorists who fire thousands of missiles at its population centres, mobs take to the streets in cities all over the world; when neighbouring countries carpet bomb civilians, the protesters stay at home. Indeed, in July 2023, when Israel responded to a wave of deadly attacks by taking out a terrorist cell in Jenin – without killing a single civilian – it received a tsunami of the most venomous hatred, with the BBC forced to apologise after a presenter insisted that 'Israeli forces are happy to kill children'.[11]

A dislike for Israel has become a core part of a suite of views held by the progressives who set the tenor of much of our culture. These 'luxury beliefs',[12] which relate to fashionable issues like race, transgenderism, decolonisation and slavery, are used as a way of signalling social status as class differences flatten, the American academic Professor Elizabeth Currid-Halkett has suggested.[13] This blend of patrician liberalism, globalism and old-fashioned socialism often comes with the kind of focus on race that is normally seen only on the far right.

As one of these social signifiers, the Israel–Palestinian conflict receives disproportionate attention. It's not just about human suffering. In 2022, about 180 Palestinian combatants and civilians lost their lives,[14] compared to

120,000 Ukrainians[15] and three thousand Yemenis killed or injured in the same period.[16] Yet between January and April 2023, the Twitter account of human rights NGO Amnesty UK – a progressive redoubt – posted no tweets at all about Yemen, two about the war in Ukraine, six about Taliban oppression in Afghanistan, seven about the brutal crack-downs in Iran, and twenty-six about Israeli 'apartheid' and other supposed crimes.

The pipeline to this milieu often begins at university, where anti-Israel orthodoxy is spread by both academics and students. On campus, fighting the bogeyman of the Jewish state has become the most desirable of causes, unmoved by the facts or a sense of proportion, a central plank in this new progressive credo. At universities in Britain, the United States and elsewhere, Jewish students and Israeli speakers are regularly bullied. In 2021, viral footage showed the Israeli Ambassador to Britain hurrying from the London School of Economics, pursued by a baying mob. Tellingly, among the activist groups that agitated against her visit was 'Decolonising LSE'.[17] On the other side of the Atlantic, students at the University of Michigan marched through the campus in January 2023 chanting 'Intifada, intifada, long live the intifada', and 'there's only one solution: intifada revolution'.[18] The two intifadas were periods of bloodshed that claimed large numbers of lives in the real world, six thousand miles away from the comfort of the University of Michigan.

In the 1960s, fewer than half of British academics were left-wing;[19] by the 2019 election, 10 per cent supported the right, while 80 per cent voted for the left.[20] The trend has been even more dramatic in the United States, where left-wing academics now outnumber those on the right by ten or fifteen to one, particularly in the humanities.[21] Nearly 40 per cent of the best liberal arts colleges have no Republicans at all, or a negligible number.[22] A 2021 study of Britain, the United States and Canada found that 'a significant portion of academics discriminate against conservatives in hiring, promotion, grants and publications' and 'right-leaning academics experience a high level of institutional authoritarianism and peer pressure'.[23] Since 2015, there has been a dramatic rise in the number of American academics – including the celebrated, left-leaning Jewish psychologist Steven Pinker[24] – who have been targeted after making remarks that do not conform to the exacting standards of progressivism.[25] Anti-Israel prejudice has become one of those standards.

Jewish students have looked on while their universities have become increasingly hostile. Ever since 2005, Israeli Apartheid Week has been marked annually on campuses worldwide, with rallies, speeches, film screenings and mock checkpoints outside libraries. Meanwhile, tens of thousands of Muslim Rohingyas have been butchered in Myanmar and women and girls raped. There was no Myanmar Apartheid Week for them; and, for that matter, no Syria Apartheid Week for those who were massacred by Assad, some with chemical weapons. Despite China's ongoing persecution of its Muslim community and vicious occupation of Tibet, there has been no Chinese Apartheid Week, even though rising numbers of Chinese students attend universities in the west. There is no comparable week of activism to condemn

Iran's massacre of democracy activists, nor North Korea's brutalisation of Christians, nor Saudi Arabia's abduction and murder of dissidents, nor Turkey's oppression of the Kurds and occupation of northern Cyprus, nor Russia's gruesome invasion of Ukraine. It comes as no surprise that declining numbers of Jews are joining the most ideological Ivy League universities,[26] many of which turn a blind eye to their ill-treatment, ignoring their protections under civil rights law.[27]

Up is down

Those who proliferate this prejudice may have no idea they're doing so. But in truth, antisemites have rarely possessed the ability to see into their own hearts. In medieval times, punishment of the Christ-killers was figured as a sacred mission, and in the twentieth century, when antisemitism was a matter of race, it claimed the moral high ground using the cover of pseudo-science. As the German philosopher Hannah Arendt observed, SS officers were told they were acting for the good of humanity because they were exterminating a biologically inferior people. They saw themselves as heroes, taking on the most gruesome of jobs for the sake of the future of the world.

The way these upside-down morals grew to encompass every corner of wartime German society provides a cautionary tale. In one of the most powerful passages in all of Arendt's writing, she concludes:

> Just as the law in civilised countries assumes that the voice of conscience tells everybody thou shalt not kill, even though

> man's natural desires and inclinations may at times be murderous, so the law of Hitler's land demanded that the voice of conscience tell everybody, thou shalt kill, although they know full well that murder is against the normal desires of most people. Evil in the Third Reich had lost the quality by which most people recognise it – that of temptation. Many Germans and Nazis, probably most of them, must have been tempted not to murder, rob, or let their neighbours go off to their doom (even though they may have been ignorant of the gruesome details of how this was achieved), and not to become accomplices in all these crimes by benefiting from them. But, God knows, they learned how to resist temptation.[28]

Far be it from me to make comparisons to the Nazis. But today's prejudice against Israel comes with its own ability to upend common decency – though via progressive politics rather than religion or pseudo-science – and to filter this distortion into wider society. Under its growing influence, hard-left activists even find themselves making common cause with the world's worst dictatorships, which stand against every principle of freedom and pluralism, to attack a democracy that while troubled and messy, protects the rights of women, gay people and minorities. Such hypocrisy is an explicit tenet of some socialist thought. The British activist John Rees – a leading figure in both the Stop the War Coalition and the Socialist Workers Party – spelled it out in black and white. 'Socialists should unconditionally stand with the oppressed against the oppressor, even if [the oppressed] are undemocratic and persecute minorities, as

Saddam Hussein persecutes Kurds and Castro persecutes gays,'[29] he wrote in 1994.

Following this creed, prominent leftists have been observed developing friendly ties with Assad's Syria, Putin's Russia and the Iranian regime, not to mention Islamist terror groups like Hezbollah and Hamas. More moderate voices often hold a diluted version of this worldview. In June 2023, it emerged that Islam Alkhatib, a student official at Goldsmiths, University of London, had tweeted: 'I clearly don't identify with the ideology Hamas promotes. However, in the event of a conflict between Israel and the Palestinians, I would take Hamas' side. (Duh).'[30]

Those on the left are not without their fellow travellers from the right. In 2013, the Belgian conservative politician Laurent Louis trampled on an Israeli flag at a Hezbollah rally in Brussels and told Syrian television that Europe was being manipulated by 'Israel, the rogue state'.[31] But the attitude is more common on the left. Driven by this moral inversion, increasing numbers of progressives feel in their heart of hearts that Hamas – racist fanatics who blow up women and children in suicide attacks, forcibly impose a repressive version of Islam, drag suspected informants behind motorbikes, shoot gays and torture and execute their rivals – are acting out of revolutionary heroism, like Che Guevara or Robin Hood.

I completely agree with you

It can be uncomfortable to acknowledge, but the claims to 'love death', made by Mohammed Hijab through a megaphone that day in central London, reflected a segment of Arab culture that sacralises a cult of bloodshed. Children on the West Bank, and especially in Gaza, are subjected to potent brainwashing, encouraged to chant praise to terrorist 'martyrs', play-act the murder of Jews and march to genocidal songs. In January 2023, when seven people – including a newly married couple, an elderly man and a fourteen-year-old-boy – were gunned down in a Jerusalem synagogue, Palestinian crowds poured into the streets, handing out sweets, singing and dancing deliriously.[32] An elaborate firework display lit the skies of Arab east Jerusalem; one man filmed himself intimidating a Jewish man in an elevator by singing songs that lionised the murders.

Such jubilation is common in the Arab world whenever Jews are killed. In 2019, Arafat Irafaiya, who knifed nineteen-year-old Ori Ansbacher to death while raping her, told police: 'I made my parents very proud of what I did. I didn't just rape someone, I murdered a Jewish woman. You won't be able to understand it because our thinking is different . . . I have done everything that Arabs dream of doing.' He added: 'If I had died during the attempt to kill more Jews, for me it is a blessed thing because then I would have died as a martyr.' Sadly, this is far from unusual. Dozens of trees planted in Ori's memory were later destroyed by Palestinians.[33]

It would be eccentric to claim that such adulation of death is not at least part of the problem. Yet despite his morbid rant and provocations, the BBC sought Hijab's wisdom a few months after the Gaza conflict for a documentary about – of all things – overcoming antisemitism. Perched uncomfortably in a deckchair in a London park, Jewish journalist Tom Brada asked him how to 'promote a sense of harmony between different communities, specifically with the Jewish community'.[34]

The British-Egyptian firebrand, who lounged in his deckchair with authority and ease, claimed that the answer lay in 'bringing people together'. He talked warmly about the Jews in his neighbourhood growing up. His family used to opt for kosher rather than halal meat, he recalled, as it adhered to the same religious standards but was of a better quality. Naturally, however, this did not extend to anybody with any sympathy for Israel. 'If someone is an apologist for Israel or for Zionism, that should be outlined or delineated or otherwise completely separated from Jewishness,' he said dogmatically. Something that Hijab did not mention – and Brada did not raise – was that at least nine out of ten British Jews are supporters of the Jewish state, cast out from Hijab's circle of trust. In other words, only 10 per cent of the community, at best, would ever be 'brought together' by this death-loving social media activist. Probably far less.

The interview also provided an insight into the sort of Jews that Hijab would be willing to embrace. When asked about his allies, the YouTuber cited the Neturei Karta, with whom he had engaged in activism in the past. At this, anybody with knowledge of the Jewish community would have reacted with a wry smile. The Neturei Karta is a marginal cult, known for its extreme theological position that Jews should not control Israel until the coming of the Messiah (though many of its members enjoy the benefits of living in the country). Described by the Anti-Defamation

League as occupying the 'farthest fringes of Judaism',[35] its small number of activists are used as mascots by the worst antisemites all over the world. Its leaders have held warm meetings with Hamas leaders in Gaza and Hezbollah chiefs in Lebanon; in 2006, its then-leader, Yisroel Dovid Weiss, attended the notorious Holocaust denial conference in Tehran.[36] I've interviewed them myself in Jerusalem for the BBC's *From Our Own Correspondent*. They are whacko.

Yet there was an obvious synergy between the secular, liberal journalist and the Muslim hardliner. It seemed that Hijab's opposition to Israel – indeed, his loathing of the place – was being given a free pass because it was 'delineated' from the hatred of Jews, so did not conform to the old notion of antisemitism. The more warmth he expressed towards 'good' Jews, the more venom he was able to express towards their national home. Shifting the target of hatred from the Jewish race to the Jewish state allowed him to duck allegations of antisemitism, opening up common ground with a small number of progressive Jews who are likewise infected with the anti-Israel prejudices of the left.

In response to Hijab's remarks about shunning the bad Jews and bonding with the good, Brada said: 'I completely agree with you, to be honest, on almost every single point.' However, he seemed unable to shake his discomfort about the interrogation of Jews on the street and asked about it again. 'We were looking for our allies and associates,' Hijab explained. 'We give voice to these voiceless pro-Palestinian Jewish people that are a big part of the Jewish community.' Those sympathetic to the 'Israeli narrative' should not be 'protected', he added, insisting that 'they should be brave enough to be cross-examined, scrutinised or otherwise interrogated publicly.'

As I watched that interview, it occurred to me that there was a common denominator between the lover of death and the liberal BBC journalist. They had reached similar ground via very different paths. The Israel to which they were relating, and which was implicitly transmitted to viewers, was a kind of Boschian vision of hell, not the real country alongside all others, with its complex mosaic of race and religion, compassion and cruelty, vice and virtue, blood and tears. That Boschian fantasy is what Hijab felt so justified in opposing with his very life, and which Brada did not find it in himself to defend.

Moreover, the ease with which the Muslim blowhard was willing to wrap his arms around those few Jews who supported him felt new. It was old poisons decanted into new bottles,[37] resembling a kind of phobia of Israel. Not a medicalised fear, like arachnophobia or claustrophobia – though it does exhibit signs of delusion – but rather an expression of hatred or prejudice, like homophobia or xenophobia.

Mutation

The late Rabbi Lord Jonathan Sacks said: 'In the Middle Ages, Jews were hated because of their religion. In the nineteenth and early twentieth century, they were hated because of their race. Today they are hated because of their nation-state, the state of Israel. It takes different forms, but it remains the same thing: the view that Jews have no right to exist as free and equal human beings.' This is self-evidently true.

However, this latest mutation has created a type of antisemitism that functions in a different way.

The western perspective on the Jews and their land is rooted in our cultural inheritance. For more than a thousand years, the Christian gaze has cast Jews as both the Chosen People and the 'synagogue of Satan'.[38] The Bible – described as 'the most valuable thing that this world affords' at the coronation of King Charles III – elevated the Jewish land to the Holy Land, the Jewish city to the Holy City and a Jewish preacher to the Son of God. Throughout the Middle Ages, the fetishisation of Jews, both as the killers of Christ and the children of the Divine, sat at the very foundation of western civilisation, frequently with catastrophic results.

The mixture of superstition, conspiratorial thinking, envy and disgust that Jews have faced over the centuries has been exacerbated by their achievements. When not being subjected to marginalisation and massacre, they have shown a remarkable capacity to thrive, with many becoming great scientists, artists, writers and financiers. Although representing 0.2 per cent of the world's population, Jews have accounted for at least 20 per cent of all Nobel Prize winners. When viewed through the eyes of antisemites, sometimes they have been categorised as subhuman, at other times superhuman. They have faced attempts at extermination and attempts at exploitation. There have been periods when they have received special admiration. But rarely have they been seen as just another people.

However secular a society becomes, it continues to be influenced by the old Christian psychodrama. The way in which Jewish morality, such as the Ten Commandments, was absorbed by the later religion may be part of the reason it feels natural to hold Jews to a higher standard. This can be expressed as infatuation: modern evangelical Christians, particularly in the United States, support Israel in the belief it will accelerate the Second Coming, and Israel's tech miracle, which has produced more billion-dollar startups than any other country per capita, has produced the familiar envy. On the flip side, the glee with which society latches on to Israel's fraught relationship with the Palestinians draws upon the cheating, bloodthirsty Jews of Shakespeare and Chaucer, as well as the cultural memory of Judas. For thousands of years, even into the mid-twentieth century, Jews were accused of murdering Gentile children and drinking their blood; is it any wonder that Israelis are smeared as child killers?

A study by economists Nico Voigtländer and Hans-Joachim Voth found that Germans from towns where Jews were blamed for the Black Death and burnt alive in the fourteenth century were significantly more likely to vote for the Nazis six hundred years later.[39] Remarkably, this was true even though Jews effectively vanished from Germany for four hundred years, between the fifteenth and the nineteenth century. The power of cultural inheritance cannot be overstated, especially where the Jewish people and the Bible are concerned. A similar story plays out in the Islamic world, with the demonisation of Jews in the Quran. Such is society's blindness towards antisemitism – or rather, such is our deep familiarity with it – that in the twenty-first century, a cartoon of a Jewish prime minister eating a baby[40] or building a wall with bloody corpses[41] can be dismissed as 'criticism of Israel'.

The insertion of Jewish statehood into the ecosystem of traditional antisemitism occurred decades before Israel had even come into existence. Published in 1903, the *Protocols of the Elders of Zion*, the most influential antisemitic text ever published, was a hoax document claiming to be written at the first Zionist Congress in 1897, the formal launch of the movement that led to the establishment of Israel. It purported to reveal a dark plot for Jews to infiltrate governments, the Church and the media in order to foment wars and revolution, and enable the rise of a world empire ruled by a Davidic dictator. In a trope that would become familiar, it portrayed the Jewish desire for self-determination as a plot to take over the world. Adapted from an 1864 satire attacking Napoleon III and an 1868 German antisemitic novel, it was designed to provoke antisemitism within Russia, where tsardom was threatened by Jewish Bolsheviks. Even in the twenty-first century, it continues to inform conspiratorial, antisemitic thinking, including modern attitudes towards Israel and the 'Zionist lobby'.

Today, the exaggerated significance of the Jewish state allows it to be painted as a unique global threat, which manipulates governments and financial markets and must be resisted by all people of conscience. On the left, it is natural to react to injustice by campaigning. But the version of Israel hallucinated by progressives is a grotesque caricature superimposed over a real country, so anti-racist energy is poured into hateful channels.

One of the innovations of modern antisemitism is to camouflage itself inside the social justice movement, turning the western conscience against its own values. This self-sabotage has a long precedent on the left. In 1940, George Orwell wrote: 'All through the critical years, many left-wingers were chipping away at English morale, trying to spread an outlook that was sometimes squashily pacifist, sometimes violently pro-Russian, but always anti-British.'[42] As Britain, the United States and other free countries share the foundations of liberal democracy with Israel, attacking western history, values and culture often goes hand in hand with attacking the Jewish state.

This is a deceitful new form of the oldest hatred. It is part of a broader social movement, fuelled not by religion or racial ideology but by a cultish conviction in its own politics. It sidesteps the old photofits by wearing a new mask, making it harder to catch. And as part of a drive to undermine the values of a free society while posing as an expression of them, it provides a template for silencing opponents. If Israel and its friends are targeted in a witch-hunt, so are other racial and sexual groups, religious believers, and those with dissenting political views or unfashionable values. Calling it antisemitism is no longer enough, as that definition remains anchored in the race-based hatred of the last century. This new bigotry, by contrast, is primarily political, enabling it to recruit progressive Jews as alibis. It is vital to find a new way to identify and respond to this new intolerance. It begins by giving it a name: Israelophobia.

Chapter Two

WHAT IS ISRAELOPHOBIA?

Israelophobia is a form of antisemitism that fixates on the Jewish state, rather than the Jewish race or religion. It cloaks old bigoted tropes in the new language of anti-racism and presents hatred as virtue. It rests on propaganda that was invented by the Nazis and Soviets; and as a political rather than racial phenomenon, it can more easily recruit small numbers of like-minded Jews. It has become the main expression of antisemitism today.

Broadly speaking, Israelophobia has three characteristics, though not all may always be present. They are:

1. **DEMONISATION** Smearing Israel as evil and a threat to the world.

2. **WEAPONISATION** Using the social justice movement as a Trojan horse for hatred of Jews and their national home.

3. **FALSIFICATION** Parroting the lies of Nazi or Soviet propaganda.

Symptoms of Israelophobia can have a range of severity. Mild sufferers may have absorbed the delusion via osmosis while conforming to the norms of their political milieu; more serious cases may have developed a devotion to the ideology and uphold it as a heartfelt, moral crusade. Either way, it has become very hard to expose, because the hatred of Jews has moved on faster than our understanding of it. Although this redux bigotry is the endpoint of two thousand years of antisemitism, it is adept at sidestepping the old labels. We've all heard the voice of the defence: 'How dare you call me antisemitic? I've been an anti-racist all my life. Look at my Jewish allies. You're just smearing me to stifle criticism of Israel.'

In this way, Jeremy Corbyn was able to demonstrate his affection for the Jewish community by attending a Passover meal with Jewdas, a hard-left, ultra-fringe organisation that has called Israel 'a steaming pile of sewage which needs to be properly disposed of'.[1] Embracing eccentric Jewish leftists as cover while pouring bile onto their national home, and spouting anti-racist rhetoric all the while, is a hallmark of Israelophobia.

Before exploring the contours of this new label further, it is necessary to pin down the meaning of an old one. One of the great achievements of the Israelophobic movement has been to give the term 'Zionist' negative connotations, grouping it with 'white supremacy' or 'colonialism'. In reality, it refers simply to the desire of the Jewish people for self-determination in their homeland, after centuries of persecution in the diaspora. As the Austro-Hungarian journalist Theodor Herzl wrote in his 1896 manifesto *Der Judenstaat*, often seen as the founding document of Zionism: 'We are a people – one people. We have sincerely tried everywhere to merge with the national communities in which we live, seeking only to preserve the faith of our fathers. It is not permitted us.' He concluded: 'The Jews who will it shall achieve their State. We shall live at last as free men on our own soil, and in our own homes peacefully die.'[2]

From one point of view, Zionism was not unusual. It was simply one expression of the nationalism that arose as the empires of the Ottomans, Austro-Hungarians, Russians and eventually the western powers gave way to new nation-states from the end of the First World War onwards. In the turbulence of those decades, imperial Britain, France, the United States and Russia made territorial pledges to many different peoples. Some came to pass; others, like those made to the Armenians and the Kurds, did not. Jewish national aspirations, however, held a particular power because of the centuries of appalling persecution they had faced, combined with the unique ancientness of their yearning for a return to their homeland.

Although the term 'Zionism' was coined in 1890 – ten years after 'antisemitism' had come into usage – the idea as a modern political force had been long in formation. In George Eliot's 1876 novel *Daniel Deronda*, the eponymous hero, who is Jewish, speaks of his commitment to such beliefs. 'The idea that I am possessed with is that of restoring a political existence to my people, making them a nation again, giving them a national centre, such as the English has, though they too are scattered over the face of the globe,' Deronda says. 'That is a task which presents itself to me as a duty; I am resolved to begin it, however feebly. I am resolved to devote my life to it. At the least, I may awaken a movement in other minds, such as has been awakened in my own.'

Its roots are older still. There were attempts to resettle Jewish people in their ancestral lands as early as 1561, around the time of Shakespeare's birth, driven by an Ottoman 'court Jew' by the name of Joseph Nasi. Before that, it took the form of a religious longing for a return to Zion, which has been enshrined in Jewish identity since they were first driven out of Israel by the Babylonians, six hundred years before Christ. Now that the Jewish state has become a firm reality, the word 'Zionism' has come to mean Israeli patriotism, of the sort that is expressed by any other nationality; or a belief among its non-Israeli supporters that the country is not the epitome of evil and deserves the right to exist. Aside from this, Zionism does not imply any political affiliation. There are left-wing Zionists and right-wing Zionists, as is made clear by the varied rallies in Israel, most of which fly the national flag, despite their diametrically opposed politics.

The flipside is the other label commonly used to describe hatred of the Jewish state: 'anti-Zionism'. This is the belief that unlike other nations, Jews are not entitled to statehood, and implies that the state of Israel, which was formed according to international law, has no 'right to exist' and should be dismantled. The bigotry of the position is clear, but it is not taboo in all circles. Although, as we shall see, it is based on distortions and dog whistles, many progressives place anti-Zionism alongside anti-racism and decolonisation in a supposed fight against oppression. Jewdas, for instance, mischaracterises Zionism as a 'bankrupt ideology that exists by pillaging everything in Jewish life for the service of a settler colony'. This is a clear attempt to legitimise a desire to deprive Jews of their self-determination, painting it as an act of virtue. For this reason, once an Israel hater has dodged the label 'antisemitism', resorting to the term 'anti-Zionism' doesn't help. The debate is inevitably sucked into a row over whether anti-Zionism is antisemitic. Amid the angry hair-splitting, the obvious point – that blind prejudice against any country and its people is wrong, whether Israel or Japan or Senegal – is lost.

It's not that the terms 'antisemitism' and 'anti-Zionism' have become useless. It's just that with the latest mutation of anti-Jewish hatred, they leave part of the landscape unmapped. That is where bad things have taken refuge. To combat this, we must triangulate 'antisemitism' and 'anti-Zionism' with the third concept of 'Israelophobia'.

Chapter Three

DEMONISATION
THE FIRST CHARACTERISTIC OF ISRAELOPHOBIA

Smearing Israel as evil and a threat to the world

You're judging

Forming an opinion about any nation, let alone one as controversial as Israel, is hardly straightforward. As the twentieth century historian Margery Perham remarked of empires, it is rather like approaching an elephant with a tape measure. 'The size and shape of the object baffles us; and, being alive, it will not keep still. And what criteria should we use?'[1] That is a difficult question to answer. Not just objective facts but scales of value are refracted through an observer's character, background, beliefs, identity, taste, politics and experiences, producing conclusions as unique as the individuals who hold them.

Some may find Americans brash, while others find them pleasingly positive. Some people love the French, or the British, or the Japanese, or the Mexicans, while others cannot abide them. A Danish friend of mine, with whom I holidayed some years ago, found Israeli culture unbearably rude, while others have found it refreshingly honest. It is similar with political and moral questions. Those whose instincts and judgments align will often share a broader worldview, becoming friends or joining the same political party. Some will tend to be more damning of Britain's imperial past than, say, that of France or Spain; some object more powerfully to Australia's tough stance on migrants than others; some will particularly deplore the behaviour of either the Pakistanis or the Indians in Kashmir; some will be inclined to defend the Russians or the Iranians or the Syrians or the Chinese; and some will have stronger views than others when it comes to Israel's conflict with the Palestinians.

Holding preferences within a respectable spectrum is perfectly natural, whether that's on the transgender debate, immigration, abortion or Israel. That's not to say that everybody is equally right. There are those with whom I profoundly disagree whose views are nonetheless reasonably held. Most people's political opinions fall within the Overton window – named after the twentieth-century American analyst Joseph Overton – referring to the range of policies acceptable to the mainstream.[2] Inside that window, rambunctious disagreement is the lifeblood of any democracy, and this is no less true when it comes to the Jewish state. Indeed, Israel is more than capable of criticising itself, as the range of argumentative voices in its boisterous free press attests.

This book is by no means making a case for moral relativism, where no judgment is made about anything. Nor is it making the case for Israel, as that has been done already.[3]

Neither is it seeking to argue against the Jewish state, for there is hardly a need for that; this fashionable orthodoxy has spawned an industry of books on the subject. Rather, its mission is to make a plea for tolerance, liberalism, factual analysis and proportional judgment. It is asking for people to be reasonable. It is seeking to pinpoint the moment where debaters depart from the rounded facts, leave honest discussion behind and stray into the realms of conspiracy theory, bigotry and demonisation. That is where Israelophobia begins.

It has become alarmingly widespread. The sheer number of committed Israelophobes and the force of their disinformation, fuelled by state-sponsored propaganda past and present – from Berlin to Tehran – has established a powerful gravitational pull. This is sucking in ordinary people, especially on the left, stretching the Overton window to allow indefensible assumptions about Israel to creep into the mainstream. The result is a sort of herd immunity to common sense.

It begins with demonisation. Natan Sharansky, the Soviet dissident, activist and author who spent nine years in a Russian prison, included it as the first of his tripartite test of anti-Jewish prejudice (the other two were 'delegitimisation' and 'double standards').[4] According to the International Holocaust Remembrance Alliance definition of antisemitism, demonisation is defined as, 'making mendacious, dehumanising, demonising, or stereotypical allegations about Jews as such or the power of Jews as collective – such as, especially but not exclusively, the myth about a world Jewish conspiracy or of Jews controlling the media, economy, government or other societal institutions.' Such negative portrayals of Jews have abounded throughout history, from the horned monsters of the Middle Ages sipping the blood of Christian children, to the Rothschild bankers pulling the strings of the financial markets, to the supposedly organ-harvesting Israelis of today.

Where are your Jews?

The drip-drip of demonisation has a profound effect. A study conducted in 2012 by the German-based Friedrich Ebert Stiftung Foundation[5] showed that 63 per cent of Poles and 48 per cent of Germans thought that 'Israel is waging a war of extermination against the Palestinians,' along with 42 per cent in Britain, 41 per cent in Hungary, and 38 per cent in Italy. The situation has not improved since. A study by the European Union Agency for Fundamental Rights on the change in attitudes between 2012 and 2018[6] found that 'simply being Jewish increases people's likelihood of being faced with a sustained stream of abuse expressed in different forms, wherever they go, whatever they read and with whomever they engage'. Antisemitism, it found, was worsening across Europe, with 85 per cent of respondents considering it a 'serious problem'. It is easy to see why: they came across antisemitic statements 'on a regular basis', the study reported, including that 'Israelis behave like Nazis toward Palestinians', that 'Jews have too much power' and that 'Jews exploit Holocaust victimhood for their own purposes'. The latest update of the study was launched in January 2023 and will be published at the end of the year.[7]

These baseless beliefs mix age-old antisemitism with hostility to Israel. Bearing in mind that they can be dispelled by even the most cursory look at the evidence, to have succeeded in creating this groupthink in the mainstream is another astonishing achievement on the part of the Israelophobia movement. Different types of prejudice can be found all over the world, from Scottish nationalists harbouring hatred of all things English, to Basque separatists abhorring the Spanish, to resentments between Ethiopians and Tigrayans, but no state is loathed as deeply or by so many around the world as Israel. There are many countries in which an Israeli citizen would be lynched on sight. Taken as a metaphor, this is true of countless other environments, from student common rooms to local council chambers.

Campaigning for the Palestinians does not necessarily equate to Israelophobia, of course. It may be true that far worse human rights abuses exist all over the globe, but this is small comfort to a family from Hebron forced to wait for hours in a queue at a checkpoint, or a Palestinian mother who has lost her child to a stray Israeli bullet. People are entitled to pursue the causes that move them. Many believe that Palestinian national aspirations are as important as those of the Israelis, and supporting them is an entirely respectable cause. There are good people on that side of the argument who build a case on solid facts, though others might oppose their narrative. As Barack Obama put it: '[Y]ou can disagree with a certain policy without demonising the person who espouses it.'[8]

Moreover, there are many Arabs who despise

Israelophobia and many Palestinians who stand against it. They deserve to be recognised. The respected president of the Jordan National Red Crescent Society, Dr Mohammed al-Hadid, was instrumental in persuading the International Committee of the Red Cross to recognise Israel's Magen David Adom (Red Star of David) under the Geneva Conventions in 2006, after it had been snubbed since its inception in 1930. And a recent damning report into antisemitism at the National Union of Students (NUS) in the UK included a statement from a Palestinian at Oxford who was appalled by the bigotry in the union. 'The advocation of Palestinian rights and valid criticism of the Israeli government should never lead to or justify racism,' he said. 'As a Palestinian, I find it deeply offensive that support for Palestinian human rights is being used to mask blatant antisemitism.'[9] Yet it remains a sad fact that many in the pro-Palestine camp have slid into the crevasse of Israelophobia.

It begins with demonisation. In their preoccupation with the evils of the Jewish state, Israelophobes will remain unmoved by the atrocities of far more deplorable regimes. Persecution throughout the Middle East, for example, has led to the Christian population in the region falling from 20 per cent a century ago to less than 4 per cent today.[10] These outrages simply don't have the same purchase on their passions.

Ironically, many of the world's crimes happen on Israel's doorstep. The Jewish state, with its 20 per cent Arab minority, is often accused of 'apartheid', while nobody mentions the fact that in many parts of the Arab world it is impossible to live as a Jew without being bullied, expelled or murdered by a mob. Israelophobes remain incensed about the 700,000 Palestinians[11] who fled their homes during Israel's turbulent War of Independence, some through fear or incompetent leadership, others through force. Yet they turn a blind eye to the 900,000 Jews who were systematically expelled from Muslim countries in the same period.[12]

Today, about half of Israel's Jewish population are from Middle Eastern families, most of whom were refugees from Islamic lands, losing their homes, communities, heritage and possessions in the process.[13] Ironically, their arrival in Israel in the 1940s and '50s helped establish the Jewish state as a viable country; it also helps explain its increasingly Middle Eastern nature, reflected in the Abraham Accords peace deals between Israel and several Arab countries, signed in 2020. Some of these families had been in Muslim countries for over a thousand years; in former times, their members had been nicknamed 'Yahud, awlad Arab' or 'Jews, sons of Arabs'. Fast forward to the present, however, and places like Lebanon, Egypt, Jordan, Syria and Iraq are home to fewer than a hundred Jews each, with some thought to have only three or four. These are countries that had thriving communities of hundreds of thousands before they were driven out.[14]

In 2017, a video of a debate at the United Nations Human Rights Council (UNHRC) went viral. One by one, diplomats from different Arab autocracies were seen lining up to accuse Israel of 'ethnic cleansing', 'terrorism', 'discrimination', 'extremism', 'crimes against humanity' and 'apartheid'. At the end, the Canadian international lawyer Hillel Neuer was given the floor. 'Once upon a time, the Middle East was full of Jews,' he said. 'Algeria had 140,000 Jews. Algeria, where are your Jews? Egypt used to have seventy-five thousand Jews. Where are your Jews? Syria, you had tens of thousands of Jews. Where are your Jews? Iraq, you had over 135,000 Jews. Where are your Jews?' He concluded: 'Mr President, where is the real apartheid?' Faced with its own hypocrisy, the debating chamber was stunned into embarrassed silence.[15]

The happy place

If the demonised version of Israel is to be replaced with the reality, the country must be seated appropriately in the family of nations. In many ways, it is an unremarkable, mid-ranking state. Geographically, it is about the size of El Salvador, Slovenia or Wales, with a population the size of New Jersey and an economy the size of Nigeria. In terms of democracy,[16] transparency[17] and quality of life,[18] it hovers in the top third of most internationally recognised league tables (though it dramatically out-performs the other countries in the region).

The Jewish state is blessed with an extremely low crime rate, ranking 104th in the world. Britain, by comparison, comes sixty-fourth, the United States fifty-sixth, France forty-fourth and South Africa third (top of the list is Venezuela).[19] Contrary to common perception, in 2022 an American insurance firm named Israel the fifth-safest tourist destination on Earth, behind only Singapore, Denmark, the Netherlands and Switzerland.[20] Its history may be bloody, but there are at least twenty-seven live conflicts in the world, affecting two billion people; and while the US-led invasions of Afghanistan and Iraq and the Syrian civil war killed several hundred thousand apiece, as did several other conflicts, like the recent appalling wars in Ethiopia and Sudan, the cumulative number of Arabs who have lost their lives in all wars with Israel numbers about 86,000.[21] That's over a period of seventy-five years.

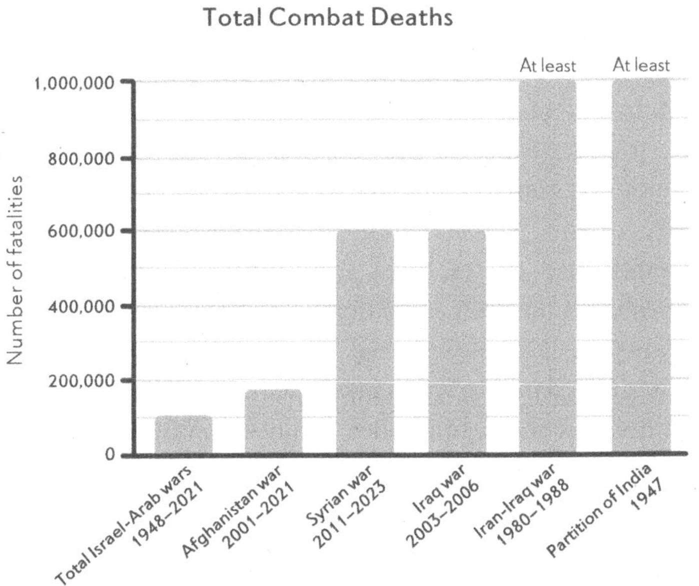

For all its problems, Israel protects the rights of women and minorities, as well as freedoms of religion, expression, assembly and so forth. In January 2023, a study by the Index on Censorship ranked the Jewish state above Britain and the United States in terms of freedom of expression.[22] Tel Aviv is one of the gay capitals of the world. In 2020, the funeral of Ayman Safiah, an openly homosexual Arab ballet dancer who drowned off the coast of Kibbutz Neve Yam, was attended by thousands of mourners in northern Israel;[23] this would be unimaginable anywhere else in the region. (In Egypt, just across the border, undercover police officers infiltrate dating apps to expose and arrest gay people, according to the BBC.)[24]

Add to these the fact that the Jewish state is a global leader in tech and has one of the best health systems in the world, with treatment even offered to the families of terrorist leaders, and its position in the UN's World Happiness Index[25] should not, perhaps, be a surprise. Top of the happy list are three of the Nordic countries, Finland, Denmark and Iceland; then comes Israel at number four. The United States ranks fifteenth and Britain nineteenth. As for Israel's neighbours, Jordan is ranked 123rd and Lebanon 136th, while latest data for Syria ranks it at 149th. The Palestinian Territories score slightly better, at ninety-ninth.

That is not to make the sort of argument that excuses Mussolini's fascism because he had the trains running on time. The fact is that in terms of freedom, democracy and quality of life, Israel is the best place in the Middle East to be a Muslim Arab, let alone a Christian or a Jew. According to a 2019 survey by the leading pollsters Dahlia Scheindlin and David Reis,[26] 76 per cent of Israeli Arabs felt that Jewish-Muslim relations were generally positive (though this was skewed slightly by age; 80 per cent of those over thirty-five replied positively, compared to 67 per cent of people between the ages of eighteen and twenty-four). Ninety-four per cent of Israeli Arabs recognised both peoples. And a recent study by the Palestinian Centre for Policy and Survey Research found that between 2010 and 2022, the percentage of Arabs living in Israeli-administered east Jerusalem who would prefer to be governed by the Palestinian Authority dropped from 52 to just 38.[27]

At the same time, no balanced observer could discount Israel's shadow side. In many ways, the country is a social and political mess. As President Reuven Rivlin said in a seminal 2015 speech, its population separates into four 'tribes' – secular Jews, religious nationalist Jews, strictly Orthodox Jews and Arabs – that are constantly pulling in different directions.[28] 'One tribe, the Arabs, whether or not by its own choice, is not really a partner in the game,' he said. 'The other three, it seems, are absorbed by a struggle for survival, a struggle over budgets and resources for education, housing, or infrastructure.'

In addition, the country is embroiled in controversies involving territorial disputes, extremism, religious chauvinism, brutality and grinding asymmetrical conflict. It is a young democracy with no constitution, a single chamber of parliament and an overly powerful supreme court, an ill-formed system that caused profound instability in 2023. Its establishment was preceded by a bloody cycle of violence between Arab and Jewish militias and British imperial forces; in the conflagration that followed, Israeli forces carried out a string of massacres that killed eight hundred prisoners of war and civilians, according to historian Benny Morris.[29] Overall, thousands of Arabs and Jews lost their lives and hundreds of thousands of Palestinians were displaced.

Critical friends

It is important to recognise that Israelophobia is not a necessary part of criticising the Jewish state. Even Edward Said, the leading anti-Israel intellectual of the twentieth century, was seen by the lawyer and antisemitism expert Anthony Julius as landing on the right side of the line, as he resisted conspiracy theories, antisemitic tropes and Holocaust denial.[30] The fact that he made a number of false anti-Israel claims,[31] dismissed the evidence of historians and myopically painted the Palestinian Arabs as victims of western imperialism disqualified him in the eyes of others. But the fact remains that reasonable criticism is entirely possible.

One area of particular concern is the Israeli government's policies towards its own Arab citizens. According to Israel's Central Bureau of Statistics, an Arab child receives a smaller education budget than a Jewish one,[32] meaning that bright, Arab-Israeli school leavers are less likely to win a place at Israeli universities, often opting to study on the West Bank or in Jordan instead. The reasons for this are complex and not explained simply by discrimination, but if the growing social divide is to be reversed, a wide-ranging package of economic and social stimulus is urgently needed for these communities, many of which are deprived. In my view, more needs to be done to better integrate Arab Israelis into mainstream society, to bring down soaring levels of crime in their communities and foster a broader sense of national identity.

Similarly, the behaviour of fringe Jewish extremists – who came to the political foreground when Benjamin Netanyahu came to power in 2022 via a coalition with the far-right – is worthy of severe condemnation. The country was shocked when Jewish thugs stalked through the Palestinian village of Huwara in February 2023, avenging a terror attack by torching cars and damaging property. An innocent man who had just returned from humanitarian work at the scene of an earthquake in Turkey was killed by gunfire during the rampage.[33] These and other criticisms can be articulated in the same way as they would of other nations, without the demonisation that acts as a springboard for Israelophobia.

When a video of Israeli police brutality circulates online, many seize it as a chance to denigrate the country itself as racist or white supremacist rather than condemning the officers responsible. By comparison, Britain's police service has been recently exposed for its misogyny, racism and malpractice, as exemplified by the murder of a woman by one serving officer and the rape of many more by another. Of the three thousand children humiliatingly strip-searched by British police in the past four years, black children were six times more likely to be targeted, figures revealed in March 2023.[34] In 2022, a black teenage girl said she would sue her school and the Metropolitan Police after she was pulled out of class and forced to remove her sanitary towel in a fruitless search for drugs.[35] In France, meanwhile, President Macron vowed to reform the police after four white officers were caught on camera beating up an unarmed black music producer in his Paris studio in 2020.[36] The tarnished record of American policing speaks for itself. Yet the foundations of these states are not questioned.

Donald Trump's election as President of the United States precipitated four years of turbulence and soul-searching. But even in that febrile period, despite the colonialism and ethnic cleansing on which the country had been founded, nobody sensible compared it to rogue regimes. The US enforced racial segregation for almost a century. The Jim Crow system – named after a disparaging term for blacks – truly was a form of apartheid. In the '50s, while the United States segregated blacks on buses and in public places, extending the spirit of bigotry that had dominated its bloody foundation, its 'right to exist' was never debated. But in those very same years, Israel's nationhood was repeatedly denied, even though it extended equal rights to its Arab minority.

Similar allegations have not been levelled at any of the other democracies that have pursued far more discriminatory policies than Israel, or fallen under the sway of the far-right. In October 2022, the Sweden Democrats – the biggest party in the world that has Nazi roots – joined that country's governing coalition, giving it influence over policymaking. Germany's Alternative Für Deutschland, with its nativist flavour, has veered between being the fifth-largest and third-largest party in the country. Italy is now led by Giorgia Meloni, also labelled by many as far-right (though others disagree). Rassemblement National, formerly Marine Le Pen's Front National, is France's largest parliamentary opposition group in the National Assembly, with a strong presence in the European Parliament.

Although the success of these political movements may speak of worrying currents within their societies, the countries themselves are not portrayed as racist. When far-right figures broke into Israel's government, however, an article in the *Times of London* compared them to the Taliban and the Ayatollahs.[37] Israel has a dark side, to be sure. But it should be perfectly possible to debate, criticise and campaign against it without resorting to demonisation. As Ze'ev Jabotinsky, one of the most significant figures in the drive to create modern Israel, wrote in 1911: 'We are a people as all other peoples; we do not have any intentions to be better than the rest. As one of the first conditions for equality we demand the right to have our own villains, exactly as other people have them.'[38]

There's bad and there's bad

The United Nations Human Rights Council (UNHRC) was founded to address human rights abuses around the globe. Yet the Jewish state, whose population is a seventh of that of Britain, has been officially condemned more than twice as often as any other nation. At the UN General Assembly, meanwhile, there were fifteen resolutions about Israel in 2022 and just thirteen about all other countries in the world combined.[39]

The UN has no fewer than seven formal bodies investigating Israel, including the Division for Palestinian Rights; the Committee on the Exercise of the Inalienable Rights of the Palestinian People; the United Nations Information System on the Question of Palestine; the Special Rapporteur on the situation of human rights in the Palestinian territories occupied since 1967; the Special Committee to Investigate Israeli

Practices Affecting the Human Rights of the Palestinian People and Other Arabs of the Occupied Territories; and the United Nations Register of Damage Caused by the Construction of the Wall in the Occupied Palestinian Territory.[40]

This didn't happen by accident. The very structure of the UNHRC was set up to produce such demonisation. Its rules dictate that Item Seven, which addresses the 'human rights situation in Palestine',[41] must be discussed at every single meeting, regardless of other pressing world affairs. No other subject is permanently on the agenda, and as a result, its conferences enter the realm of absurdity. In 2019, at its forty-first convocation in Geneva, activists rallied outside to demand an end to the genocide of the Uighurs while delegates discussed the 'rise in hate speech by political representatives and on social media in Israel'.[42] Setting aside the deep irony of the fact that Israel is by far the most maligned country in the world on social media,[43] it was grotesque to see tweets by Israeli politicians eclipsing the genocide of Muslims in China.

It has been this way for years. The UN's notorious 2001 anti-racism conference in Durban famously descended into naked Jew-hatred.[44] When it was convened again, in 2009, the only head of state to speak was the Iranian president, Mahmoud Ahmadinejad. In his speech, he smeared Israel as 'totally racist', called the Holocaust an 'ambiguous and dubious question' and claimed it was used as a 'pretext' for oppressing Palestinians.[45] In his recent memoir, Danny Danon, Israel's former ambassador to the UN, recalls his first days in the job. 'I knew about the hostility at the UN and I was prepared for that,' he writes, 'but nobody can prepare for the volume of attacks against Israel. Some weeks we had to deal with a new crisis every day, such as resolutions, initiatives and reports. So basically, you end up working day and night to defend your position.'[46]

In May 2023, despite the fact that the UN had itself voted to establish the Jewish state in 1947, the organisation staged an event to commemorate the 'catastrophe' of Israel's birth. At this carnival of Israelophobia, Mahmoud Abbas, the Palestinian leader, was allowed to give a speech lasting twice his allotted time of thirty minutes (though to be fair, he is currently enjoying the eighteenth year of his four-year term in office). He railed against the Jewish state in the most lurid terms. Attempting to deny the historical fact that Jewish agriculturalists made the wasteland of Palestine bloom in the early twentieth century – before their time, in 1867, Mark Twain had described the country as 'a silent mournful expanse'[47] – Abbas even wheeled out a Nazi metaphor. 'They lie and lie, just like Goebbels,' he ranted. 'They lie, lie and lie until people believe.'[48]

It's a simple thought experiment, but let's imagine that it wasn't Israel but China. By any criteria, China's record on human rights, corruption and destabilisation overseas dwarfs that of Israel. Its clampdown on Hong Kong has been brutal and at the time of writing there are fears that it may invade its democratic neighbour, Taiwan, plunging the region into war. It was the source of the Covid pandemic. It has an appalling record on occupation; since the People's Republic invaded Tibet in 1949, whole communities have been wiped out, monasteries have been destroyed and the country has been subjected to an oppressive regime. The US think-tank Freedom House now ranks Tibet among the worst places in the world for civil rights and political freedom.[49] And China presents a very real, direct and intensifying threat to the west.

Nonetheless, imagine for a moment if the People's Republic was the only state to be debated at every UNHRC gathering and had been condemned more than twice as many times as any other country. Imagine there was a widespread campaign to boycott Chinese goods, academics, sports teams, musicians and dance troupes. Imagine if Chinese students at universities were victimised, bullied and accused by their own lecturers of being agents of a 'violent, racist, foreign regime engaged in ethnic cleansing',[50] with their own student unions amplifying this hatred. Who are these people, you'd ask yourself, and why are they demonising China?

Some say that higher standards are expected of a western-style democracy. But that does not explain why the Jewish state is scrutinised, criticised and undermined so much more than the United States, Australia, France or Britain; and it certainly does not explain why it is treated as if it was far more malign than the autocracies.

History and hummus

Portraying Israel as a colonial imposition on indigenous people, a 'settler-state' expropriating their land and culture, is a major pillar of Israelophobia. It is rooted in the suggestion that Jews have no place in the Middle East and are alien to the region, a claim that is easily dismissed with even the briefest look at history. Yet the demonisation persists.

Take Akub, a fashionable Palestinian restaurant in

London's Notting Hill. It is more than just a high-end eatery. In an interview with the *New York Times* in 2022, its French-trained chef and founder, Fadi Kattan, said his mission was to 'reclaim a cuisine that is part of a broader Arab tradition involving foods like hummus, falafel, tabbouleh, fattoush and shawarma, that he felt was being co-opted by Israeli cooks'.[51] It seems that whereas normal people *cook* food, in the eyes of Kattan, Israelis 'co-opt' it. This position relies on a highly selective view of history. As one reader remarked in the comments section: 'Jews have also been making these foods for centuries and have appropriated nothing. There's been a continuous Jewish presence in the land of Israel for thousands of years. What's more, many of these foods are not limited to the land of Israel, but common across the former Ottoman empire.'

People often forget that Judaism is two millennia older than Islam and 1,500 years older than Christianity. Israel was the cradle of Jewish civilisation. At least a thousand years before the birth of Jesus Christ, Jerusalem's most famous Jew, King David, made the city the capital of the Land of Israel. It has been home to greater or lesser numbers of Jews – the very word 'Jew' is a shortening of Judea, the ancient kingdom radiating from Jerusalem in the Iron Age – in Jerusalem ever since.

Culturally, Jews have always intertwined their identity with the land of Israel, particularly since they were exiled to Babylon around 598 BC, when their powerful yearning for return took hold. For millennia, Jews in the diaspora have prayed facing towards the Holy City; exclaimed 'next year in Jerusalem' at Passover; mourned the destruction of the

Temple by breaking a glass at weddings and leaving a corner of their homes undecorated; longed to be buried there; prayed at the remaining walls of the destroyed Temple; and visited on pilgrimage. Many throughout history have taken the step of uprooting their families and returning to their homeland. All these practices continue to this day.

A thread can be traced backwards through Jewish history that shows the ancient roots of the ideal of repatriation. Beginning in 1516, Palestine – as it had been renamed by the Romans – fell under Ottoman rule, which would last for more than four hundred years. Less than fifty years after the conquest, Joseph Nasi, the Duke of Naxos, a Portuguese Jewish diplomat favoured by the Ottomans, attempted to return Jews to their homeland without regard for scriptural prophecies about awaiting the coming of the Messiah. In a way, he was the first Zionist.

The fortunes of the Jews of the Holy Land rose and fell over the following centuries. In 1860, the British financier Sir Moses Montefiore, who believed in the divine providence of the British empire and the Jewish return to Zion, founded the community of Mishkenot Sha'ananim just outside the Old City of Jerusalem. Composed of red-brick alms houses and a windmill, it was the earliest forerunner of the future state (the windmill still stands today).

Modern Jewish migration to Palestine began in 1883 with an influx of 25,000 Jewish arrivals, many fleeing antisemitic mobs in Russia and inspired by a desire to return to their ancestral lands. Jews also came from as far afield as Persia and Yemen, grouping into their own neighbourhoods. Immigrants from Bukhara, Uzbekistan, including the Moussaieff family of jewellers who had cut diamonds for Genghis Khan, created the Bukharan Quarter (Shkhunat HaBucharim), with its distinctly central Asian feel. Their imperative to return had been building for thousands of years.

Writing in the *Jewish Chronicle* in 1896, Herzl, the father of modern Israel, laid out the concept of Zionism. 'I am introducing no new idea,' he pointed out. 'On the contrary, it is a very old one. It is a universal idea – and therein lies its power – old as the people, which never, even in the time of bitterest calamity, ceased to cherish it. This is the restoration of the Jewish State.' He added: 'It is remarkable that we Jews should have dreamt this kingly dream all through the long night of our history. Now day is dawning. We need only rub the sleep out of our eyes, stretch our limbs, and convert the dream into a reality.'[52] Eighteen months later, in 1897, came the famous first Zionist Congress in Basel. Afterwards, Herzl wrote in his diary: 'L'état c'est moi. At Basel, I founded the Jewish state. If I said this out loud today, I would be greeted by universal laughter. Perhaps in five years and certainly in fifty, everyone will know it.'[53]

A new beginning

Four further waves of immigration followed, as Jews fled butchery around the world for Ottoman-controlled Palestine. By 1896, more than three-fifths of the 45,300 residents of Jerusalem were Jewish.[54] Yousef al-Khalidi, the mayor of the city, wrote to his old friend Zadok Khan, Chief Rabbi of France: 'Who can contest the rights of the Jews to Palestine? God knows, historically it is indeed your country.'[55] In 1915, as the contours of the future Jewish state were continuing to emerge, Palestinian Arab nationalism had yet to appear. 'Questions of Arabs and their nationality are as far from them as bimetallism from the life of Texas,' wrote Lawrence of Arabia at the time. 'Christians and Mohammedans come [to Jerusalem] on pilgrimage; Jews look to it for the political future of their race.'[56]

During the First World War, the Turks sided with the Germans. After their defeat, the Ottoman empire collapsed and huge swathes of its territory passed into the hands of the allied powers. The Ottomans had administered their territories in *vilayets*, or cantons, and these became the basis for the carve-up by the allies. In the Middle East, French Syria took three *vilayets* – Damascus, Aleppo and Beirut – which were home to Maronite Christians, Shia and Sunni Muslims, and Druze and Alawites. The French later divided the territory into Syria and Lebanon. British Iraq was created out of three *vilayets*, Baghdad, Basra and Mosul, stitching together a patchwork of Shia and Sunni Muslims, Yazidi, Kurds and Iraqi Jews. After independence, the country proved as ungovernable for the Iraqis as it had been for the British. The *vilayets* of Palestine, inhabited by Sunni and Christian Arabs, Druze, Bedouin and Jews, were placed under a British mandate, meaning that Britain would administer the territory until the inhabitants were eligible for self-government, at which time independent nation-states would be born.

Thus, in 1917, Imperial Britain became the first Christian power to rule Jerusalem for more than seven centuries. It was the fulfilment of a long-held aspiration. Prime Minister David Lloyd George famously described Jerusalem as 'a

Christmas present for the British people', having exclaimed, 'Oh, we must grab that!'[57] On 11 December, after routing the German-led Ottoman forces in one of the last successful cavalry charges in modern warfare, Field Marshal Edmund Allenby dismounted and entered the Holy City on foot. Britain had just issued the historic Balfour Declaration, a statement of support for a 'national home for the Jewish people' in Palestine, intended to detach Russian Jews from Bolshevism. This was typical of the tactical pledges made by the Great Powers under wartime pressure, many of which contradicted each other. Governing the mandate was not easy, as Jewish aspirations for statehood grew and tensions with the Arabs mounted; in the '30s, Palestinian nationalism was born, sparking cycles of internecine violence.

Then came the Second World War. The Holocaust deepened the case for a Jewish state, which would be able to stand its own army and fulfil the pledge 'never again'. In the manner of an indigenous people revolting against the British Empire – and sharing a common struggle with other colonised nations groaning under the imperial jackboot – Jewish guerrillas mounted an armed campaign against the British to push them out of Palestine. As had become the norm across the Middle East and Europe, in 1947, the UN agreed to partition the land into a Jewish state and a Palestinian one, with borders traced around ethnic majority areas (the *vilayets* of Jordan had been parcelled up and placed under Hashemite rule a year before). Under the terms of this two-state solution, Israel would comprise 56 per cent of the land, while the Palestinians would occupy 43 per cent. The populations would be mixed, with half-a-million Arabs on the

Israeli side, and 10,000 Jews living in the State of Palestine. Israel's neighbours reacted with dismay; they had harboured their own lust to annex the territory. On 14 May 1948, eight hours before British rule officially ended in the Tel Aviv Museum of Art on Rothschild Boulevard, David Ben-Gurion, the country's first prime minister, got to his feet and proclaimed Israel's independence. Forty-four years after Herzl's death, his prediction had come true.

The Jewish side had accepted the UN partition plan. After all, to the north, the Syrians and Lebanese had likewise agreed to be partitioned, despite much grumbling from the Alawites and Druze. But the Palestinians – led by the Mufti of Jerusalem, Amin al-Husseini, who had collaborated closely with the Third Reich during the war and, as we will see in the chapter on Falsification, relished the idea of exterminating the Jews – rejected any treaty that involved the establishment of a Jewish state. Just hours after Ben-Gurion's speech, following Husseini's lead, the armies of Egypt, Jordan, Iraq, Lebanon and Syria attacked the fledgling Jewish country. 'This will be a war of extermination and a momentous massacre,' announced Abdul Rahman Hassan Azzam, secretary-general of the Arab League, 'which will be spoken of like the Mongolian massacres and the Crusades.' The Mufti called for jihad, crying: 'Murder the Jews! Murder them all!'[58] Ironically, as the scholar Joseph Spoerl has pointed out, 'the plan for ethnic cleansing in Palestine in 1947–8 was an Arab plan, not a Zionist one'.[59]

An existential struggle ensued. Stalin, who had been the first to recognise Israel, ensured that it received invaluable Soviet armaments from Eastern Europe, and with its organised and determined fighting units – many of whom had survived the Holocaust – the Jewish state withstood the onslaught. In the chaotic *Sturm und Drang* of war, about 700,000 Arabs fled their homes. As Simon Sebag Montefiore recounted: 'Some were expelled by force, some departed to avoid the war, hoping to return later – and approximately half remained safely in their homes to become Israeli Arabs, non-Jewish citizens in the Zionist democracy'.[60] The Palestinian refugee problem, writes historian Benny Morris, '. . . arose as a product of the war, not of planning, on either the Jewish or the Arab side . . . It was partly the result of malicious actions by Jewish commanders and politicians, but to a lesser extent Arab commanders and politicians were responsible for its creation through their orders and failures.'[61] The existence of two million Arab citizens of Israel today shows how allegations of 'ethnic cleansing' have been twisted and weaponised. There are no Jews under Palestinian rule, and the Jewish communities living cheek-by-jowl with them require heavy military protection. Where is the real ethnic cleansing?

After nine months of fighting, the war ended. The 1949 Armistice Agreement, supervised by the UN, split Jerusalem and placed the Old City in the hands of King Abdullah of Transjordan, who had also succeeded in annexing the West Bank, which the UN had set aside for the Palestinians. 'Nobody will take over Jerusalem from me unless I'm killed,' he declared. The terms allowed Jews access to the Western Wall, the cemetery on the Mount of Olives and the tombs of Kidron Valley, but these pledges were never honoured. Jews were not able to visit the Wall for the next nineteen years, and their gravestones were defaced.

With an uneasy peace restored, there was a further

ingathering of the exiles. Immigrants arrived from all over the world, including many of the 900,000 Jews who had been driven out of their homes in the great antisemitic purge of Arab lands. Today, seventy-five years after the War of Independence, 80 per cent of Israeli Jews were born in Israel[62] and half of the country's Jewish population is now black or Middle Eastern, meaning that those labelled by some as 'white' are in the minority. Far from being a white supremacist state, Israel is a deeply multi-racial one.

The demonisation of Israel presents it as a unique historical evil. In truth, however, the manner of its creation was typical of the period. These historical facts show that unlike the United States, Australia or the South American countries, Israel was founded as a post-colonial state, not a colonial one, established legitimately under international law after the withdrawal of Imperial Britain. Sadly, for the remainder of the twentieth century and what we have seen of the twenty-first, the Palestinian territories and Israel – along with Iraq, Syria, Lebanon and Jordan – have been beset by typical post-colonial problems of ethnic rivalry, expulsion and unrest. The Iran–Iraq war of the 1980s alone claimed the lives of a million soldiers and the same number of civilians. Indeed, aside from the singularity of the ancient Jewish story, the Holocaust and the volume of migration from the diaspora, only two things were exceptional about Israel's birth. First, the 50 per cent of the Arab population that had remained within its borders were granted full citizenship. Second, despite its messiness, it became a liberal democracy with a strong economy, which made it unique in the region. Yet despite all this, Jews are still blamed for stealing the hummus.

Historic injustices

Customers of the Akub restaurant are served their 'reclaimed' dishes against a backdrop of rows of keys displayed on the wall. These represent the property that was lost by the 700,000 Arabs who fled when Israel was founded, fuelling demands for restitution. This is an example of the fetishisation of Palestinian dispossession, which has become one of the world's best-known historic injustices. In that same period, millions of other people were driven across borders in Europe and Asia, amid the same post-colonial turmoil, in more violent circumstances, their homes seized, their relatives killed, their cultures lost and their families fragmented; yet their stories have been buried by history.

Who laments the plight of the Greek Orthodox Christians, or the Indian Hindus and Sikhs, or the Armenians, or the Irish refugees created after the bloody British partition of 1921, or the twelve million ethnic Germans expelled from Eastern Europe on Churchill's instigation after the Second World War? Or the Jews of the Middle East, for that matter? As the Jewish food critic Giles Coren remarked: 'I know how [Fadi Kattan] feels: in the period he is talking about, my family had a department store in Bratislava. But there was an invasion, they had to leave, and now, well, yes, I would quite like to have it back. But it's not going to happen. My family didn't get to go home. Most of them were asphyxiated in gas chambers or shot in forests, some of them went to Israel/Palestine (I'm sorry about that, Fadi, I really am), and some of them came to England.'[63]

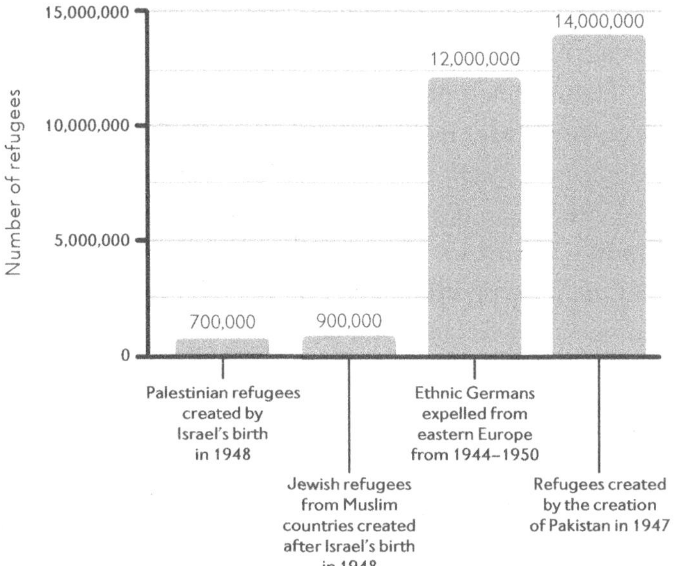

That's not to say that Israel's sins must not be condemned, or that the Palestinian injustice should be forgotten. It's simply a question of exposing demonisation. The Jewish state was born in an era when mass displacement was common. As the age of empire was replaced by the age of the nation-state, ethnic groups demanded their own independent countries. Nationalist movements surged, a typical example of which was Zionism, described by Stalin simply as 'Jewish national expression'.[64] The Ottoman, Austro-Hungarian, Russian and German empires crumbled and in the following decades, in the high-handed manner of the early twentieth century, their territories were parcelled out by Englishmen, Frenchmen and Americans, based on the ethnic makeup of the local inhabitants. The results were always the same: inter-communal violence and the mass expulsions of minorities across the new frontiers.

Many historians trace the first modern example of the nation-state to Greece, another ancient civilisation on the shores of the Mediterranean. In the 1820s, the Greeks revolted against the Ottomans, leading to the foundation of modern Greece as an Orthodox Christian kingdom. Although they had lived intermingled lives, Muslims were forced into Turkey and Orthodox Christians driven into Greece. Massacres occurred on both sides. In 1923, the European powers authorised further population transfers, aiming to create two ethnically distinct nation-states, and at least two million people were expelled along ethnic and religious lines. As late as 1965, fifty thousand Greeks were forced out of Istanbul, their property requisitioned in a process known as 'Turkification'. To this day, xenophobic sentiment lingers on both sides. There are differences, of course, but the parallels with Israel's birth are obvious.

Further afield, India and Pakistan were created in 1947, within a few months of the birth of Israel. This was likewise the result of British withdrawal and partition (though in the case of Palestine, plans for two states were rejected by the Arabs). But while the establishment of the Jewish state created 700,000 Palestinian refugees, followed by 900,000 Jewish ones, the Indian partition amounted to the largest mass migration in human history,[65] with fourteen million Muslims and Hindus displaced. In Israel's War of Independence, about 16,500 were killed;[66] in the case of India and Pakistan, at least a million were butchered, with some estimates doubling that number. Four wars followed on the Indian subcontinent and to this day, both sides, in different ways, continue to persecute their minorities. In India, Hindu nationalism menaces over 200 million Muslim citizens, while the Islamic Republic of Pakistan upholds draconian heresy laws and oppresses Shia, Sufis, Hindus, Ahmadis and Christians, not to mention women.

Both are now nuclear powers. While a cycle of conflict and stalemate dominates Israeli–Palestinian relations today, claiming about eleven thousand lives in the last two decades, in Kashmir, a violent territorial dispute has led to tens of thousands of deaths. There is even an Indian version of *Fauda* – the Israeli thriller about undercover soldiers operating in the Palestinian territories – set in Kashmir. And while Israel's human rights record holds up very well in comparison to its neighbours, that of modern Pakistan is abysmal, rife with corruption and brutality, including widespread violence against women, religious persecution and slavery (it comes 108th in the World Happiness Index). Yet you don't hear western progressives suggesting that Pakistan – or any post-colonial state aside from demonised Israel – has 'no right to exist'. And they are not targeted by street protests, boycotts, activism in international institutions or university campaigns.

Whatever the turbulence of their history, it is absurd to deny the right of Jewish Israelis to live in that land. It sometimes seems like the Israeli–Palestinian conflict is uniquely immune to the passage of time. If the early Zionists were branded 'settlers' to begin with, how many decades must pass before that label falls away? How is it possible to argue that the

80 per cent of Israelis born in that country[67] are not deserving of their national identity? Even setting aside the moral imperative that flows from the richness of Jewish history and culture in the region, such exclusionary measures are not applied to citizens of other young countries born in war.

Nor are they applied to other immigrants. Across the west, society falls over itself to adopt an open attitude towards newcomers from all over the world, whatever their countries of origin, accepting them as citizens as soon as they have a passport and making them feel at home. Concerns about ethnicity are derided as racist. In December 2022, when 83-year-old Lady Susan Hussey, one of the late Queen Elizabeth's ladies-in-waiting, asked the British-born charity executive Ngozi Fulani where she was from, Lady Hussey was forced out of her job. Those on the far-left were the first to condemn her as a bigot. They are also more likely to believe in the principle of open borders, which would allow anybody to live anywhere. When it comes to Israel, however, different standards apply.

It is revealing to compare the west's thinking on immigration to its views on Israel. Sunder Katwala, director of the British Future think-tank, asks 'how do people become us?'. One of the best barometers could be a 'full integration in one generation' test, he suggests. Then, he expresses some queasiness about the exclusionary notion of 'second-generation' and 'third-generation' immigrants. 'The children, and even the grandchildren, of migrants are often still perceived more as "them" than "us", an indicator of a persistent gap between the legal facts of equal citizenship and the social perceptions of what that really means,'[68] he writes. A perfectly reasonable point. Yet progressives continue to see Israeli Jews as the eternal 'them' in their own homeland, regardless of the generations that preceded them. Palestinians, by contrast, are the eternal 'us', retaining their 'right of return' ad infinitum, and uniquely passing their displaced status down to future generations. According to the UN, there are five times more Palestinian refugees today than there were in 1948.[69]

Next year in Palestine

It is true, of course, that the Palestinians can speak also of exile and dispossession. But the context is very different. Historically, the Jews were pushed by persecution into a desire for their own state. For centuries, the yearning for a return to Zion was a religious and cultural matter, meaning that many Jews believed that rebuilding Israel was prohibited until the arrival of the Messiah. Instead, they did their utmost to make lives for themselves throughout the diaspora, from Berlin to Baghdad, from Algeria to the furthest reaches of the Russian empire. Sometimes, they tried so hard to be accepted by society that they became more patriotic than everybody else.

In Britain the practice of singing the national anthem at Jewish bar mitzvahs and weddings only died out in the '70s, and a prayer for the monarchy is still recited every Shabbat. On Whitechapel Road, in the old Jewish East End, a memorial still stands to King Edward VII. Unveiled in 1912, a plaque on its base says it was erected 'from subscriptions raised from Jewish inhabitants of East London'. In other words, by immigrants who were falling over themselves to demonstrate loyalty to the Crown.

Yet the opportunity to be seen as truly 'us' was denied to them. Whether in the form of the Spanish Inquisition, the pogroms of the nineteenth century or the Holocaust, periods of acceptance have tended to give way to savage persecution. In the nineteenth and twentieth centuries, the plight of the Jews, this dispersed, tortured, wandering people that had been so degraded and diminished by violence, came to weigh on the consciences of world leaders. The answer that emerged from the Jews themselves was repatriation to their ancestral home in Palestine, which became a possibility once it had been left stateless by the evaporation of the Ottoman empire.

Over the preceding decades, at least thirty-four territories had been put forward as possible sanctuaries for the Jewish people, including Uganda, parts of South America, Angola, Libya, Iraq, Madagascar and Alaska. Efforts had been made to convert some of them into reality: in a move to capture Jewish national instincts within the Soviet project, Stalin had tried to establish a Jewish 'homeland' in two different locations, Birobidzhan and Crimea. Both fizzled out, proving that it was not possible to fabricate a true sense of belonging. As early as 1908, Winston Churchill had expressed his sympathy for a 'restoration' of a Jewish homeland between the Jordan River and the Mediterranean Sea. After the Holocaust, with the population of European Jewry diminished by two thirds, Zionism seemed the only solution.

The Palestinian story is very different. The UN partition plan of 1947 – presented before the War of Independence, before a single family had fled their home – proposed a State of Palestine alongside a State of Israel. But the Arabs rejected it, their ambitions for self-rule eclipsed by their abhorrence for Jewish self-determination. In truth, modern Palestinian nationalism had only arisen in response to Zionism. They are part of a much larger Arab nation, occupying a vast landmass of five million square miles across western Asia and North Africa, from the tip of Oman on the Arabian Sea to the North Atlantic coast of Morocco. There is rich variety in the Arab world, but the pan-Arab nationalist movement, which reached the height of its popularity in the 1950s and '60s, advocated a union of their lands as a post-colonial bloc. The pressures of Islamism, sectarianism, power struggles and military failure eventually fragmented the dream, but the pan-Arabist Ba'ath party, which has ruled Syria continuously since the coup of 1963 and dominated Iraq under Saddam Hussein, remains active in many countries across the Middle East. Indeed, the three attempted genocidal wars against Israel, the War of Independence, the Six Day War and the Yom Kippur War of 1973, were mounted by a coalition of Syrians, Lebanese, Jordanians, Egyptians, Iraqis and others. They are testament to the strength of a common Arab identity.

For decades, the Palestinian rejectionist stance towards Israel was aligned with that of the Arab states. It was expressed at the infamous meeting of the Arab League in Sudan in 1967, which resulted in the 'Three Noes of Khartoum': no peace with Israel, and no negotiation with Israel, and no recognition of Israel. Notwithstanding episodes like the Oslo Accords peace agreements – tragically derailed in 1995 after a Jewish extremist assassinated Israeli prime minister Yizchak Rabin – this has tended to drive the Palestinian approach. In the words of Israeli diplomat Abba Ebban, '. . . the Arabs never miss an opportunity to miss an opportunity.'[70]

None of this is to downplay the Palestinian desire for statehood, which has huge support internationally, including in Israel. It would be wonderful to see a peaceful and prosperous State of Palestine. But those desires could have been fulfilled many times over by now, including in 1948, an opportunity which – as we will examine in the chapter on Falsification – was rejected by Palestinian extremists who had come to dominate the leadership. Another revealing moment came in 2008, when after intensive negotiations, Israeli Prime Minister Ehud Olmert tabled an unprecedented offer. Its terms included: 94 per cent of the West Bank given to the Palestinians, with 6 per cent of Israeli land added to make up the difference; East Jerusalem placed under Palestinian sovereignty, making it the capital of a Palestinian state; Israel withdrawing from the Old City of Jerusalem, which would be under international administration; a tunnel connecting the West Bank and Gaza, ensuring Palestinian territorial contiguity; and Israel accepting a thousand Palestinian refugees annually for five years, with financial compensation provided for the rest. It is hard to imagine a more generous plan. Yet in a grotesque failure of leadership, Mahmoud Abbas turned it down.

Writing in the *Washington Post* the following year, Olmert said: 'It would be worth exploring the reasons that the Palestinians rejected my offer and preferred, instead, to drag their feet, avoiding real decisions.'[71] As we shall see, it is hard to resist the conclusion that Palestinian nationalism rests more on hatred of the Jews than the desire for statehood.

You do it then

Israel's track record since its establishment compares respectably to those of the other liberal democracies, even though it exists in a far tougher neighbourhood. Britain, one of the most enlightened and tolerant societies the world has ever seen, comes with deep shadows of its own. The list includes episodes like the 1919 Amritsar massacre, in which hundreds of peaceful protestors were gunned down in cold blood, and the collective punishment of half-a-million post-war Malayans by destroying their homes and interning them in fortified camps called 'New Villages'. In 2022, it emerged that the Royal Air Force had killed at least sixty-four children in Afghanistan, four times the figure that it had previously acknowledged.[72] That story was reported on the morning news in Britain but had vanished from bulletins by the evening; it was hard not to wonder what the reaction would have been had it been Israeli bombs killing Palestinians rather than British ones killing Afghans.

Similarly, the US, one of the freest countries in history, is far from perfect. Over the century leading up to its establishment, a staggering fifty-six million indigenous people were massacred. According to a recent study at University College London, the genocide caused abandoned farmland the size of France to become reforested, resulting in a drop in carbon dioxide emissions and a cooling in the temperature of the earth.[73] Years of slavery and segregation followed. In 1945, the US became the only country to have ever used nuclear weapons in conflict, killing more than two hundred thousand people in Hiroshima and Nagasaki. The Iraq invasion of 2003, which claimed hundreds of thousands of lives, brought Abu Ghraib, waterboarding, extraordinary rendition and Guantanamo Bay into the popular vocabulary. By the time the US-led Afghan campaign came to a humiliating close in 2021, the equivalent of the population of the US town of Olympia in Washington State, or Inverness in Scotland, had been wiped out in Afghan civilians alone. Yet it is Israel, not the United States, that is routinely accused of settler-colonialism, apartheid, ethnic cleansing and land theft, and is said to have 'no right to exist'.

Pointing out these double standards is not 'whataboutery'. It is a way of showing how Israel is demonised. If you read the history of any state, you will find chapters of brutality, conquest and wrongdoing, much of which dwarfs anything of which the Jewish one has been accused. French troops in Jaffa at the turn of the nineteenth century raped girls on the cadavers of their mothers.[74] In the Spanish civil war of 1936, hundreds of thousands were butchered in systematic liquidations and mob violence, with torture and rape commonplace. Framing the brutality as a 'holy war' against a 'Judeo-Masonic-Bolshevist' conspiracy, Franco's troops distributed the notorious antisemitic forgery the *Protocols of the Elders of Zion*. In 1947, as the UN voted to establish the state of Israel, Dutch colonial forces in Indonesia rounded up 431 Rawagede villagers and executed them in cold blood, in what the UN described as 'deliberate and merciless' killings.

In 1951, as the Tel Aviv Stock Exchange opened for the first time, Greenlandic children were forcibly sent to Denmark for 'Danification' by Danish colonial forces. And brutal violence and expulsions characterised the creation of new nation-states throughout the twentieth century.

While the 1950s saw an influx of Holocaust survivors and Jewish refugees from Arab and Muslim countries expand Israel's population to two million, British troops were dealing out gruesome torture on the Kikuyu people in Kenya, raping both women and men with broken bottles, gun barrels, knives, snakes, vermin and hot eggs, dragging victims behind Land Rovers, whipping, burning and bayoneting them, and conducting mass hangings and summary shootings. In 1967, as the Six Day War erupted in Israel, the US's Operation Rolling Thunder was devastating Vietnam; by its conclusion the following year, it had wiped out 180,000 civilians, to say nothing of combatants. While Israel fought the desperate Yom Kippur War in 1973 – bringing it as close to the brink of destruction as it has ever been – Pinochet seized power in Chile, sending his 'caravan of death' on a murderous tour of the country. The conclusion is unavoidable: if we were to apply the same level of hysteria towards all countries that some direct at Israel, we'd be hysterical about everything all the time.

Stuck in the middle

Today, the security challenges faced by the Jewish state eclipse those of any other comparable western democracy. It is surrounded by entities that are devoted to its destruction.

On its northern border is Hezbollah, which has a stockpile of up to 150,000 missiles – a bigger arsenal than many nation-states – and Syria, filled with Iranian troops and proxies. To its west there is the Gaza Strip, run by the terror organisation Hamas and home to several other militant groups. On its eastern flank, the Palestinian Authority territories are dysfunctional and corrupt, riddled with human rights abuses, terror cells, tribal rivalries and failing public services. To the south is the lawless Sinai desert. And further afield there is Iran, which is theologically committed to the liquidation of the Jewish state, supports a network of terrorists both on Israel's borders and throughout the region, and is on the cusp of becoming a nuclear power.

In 2022 alone, Israel was hit with more than five thousand terror attacks, ranging from assaults with rocks to stabbings, shootings and bombings. If New Jersey was uprooted and set in Israel's place, would the United States military kill fewer civilians? Would the British army, if Wales landed alongside Syria, Lebanon and Gaza? Would the French? When Britain faced terrorism from the IRA, its response was brutal. And the last time it faced a truly existential threat, during the Second World War, few aside from Church of England bishops objected to the savage firebombing of Dresden.[75] If Canada started launching rockets onto Detroit, or an independent Scotland fired missiles into England, citizens would demand a military response, even though people on the other side would die. In fact, given that the Israel Defence Force (IDF)'s combatant-to-civilian casualty ratio is less severe than that of British and US troops in recent conflicts,[76] probably *more* people on the other side would die. Yet under the influence of Israelophobia, the media routinely presents Israel's carefully calibrated acts of self-defence as aggression, while playing down the attacks it faces.

Consider, for example, how the BBC covered the conflict between Israel and Islamic Jihad in May 2023. On the World Service, the presenter said: 'To the Middle East now, where Palestinian officials say that two young men have been killed during an overnight Israeli army raid near Jenin in the occupied West Bank. It came hours after Israel carried out air strikes on Gaza, targeting militant commanders. Fifteen people were killed, including ten civilians. Israel's prime minister Benjamin Netanyahu warned Palestinian militants that any retaliation would be met with a crushing response.'

The interviewer then asked *Jerusalem Post* journalist Lahav Harkov whether the timing of Israel's attacks was significant. Tersely, she replied: 'It's significant because of details that you left out in your introduction. For example, the two Palestinian men shot in Jenin overnight were shooting at IDF soldiers and the IDF soldiers shot them back . . . The operation in Gaza came after Palestinian Islamic Jihad shot 102 rockets towards Israeli civilian centres. Then Israel took a week or so to prepare its operation and use its intelligence and then, yes, retaliated. But retaliated in a way that was commensurate with international law because they shot at civilians and Israel shot at the terrorists who were leading this organisation and this operation to shoot at civilians.'[77] This was a comprehensive rebuttal of Israelophobia with a reasonable interpretation of the facts. Sadly, commentators like Harkov are all too rare.

It is hard to overstate the demonisation that surrounds the Jewish state and colours public perception of it. It stands condemned for failing to observe the rules-based international order at a time when it was not followed by any country. It is doubly condemned for falling below standards that are upheld by nobody today, least of all those in the Middle East. Like any other nation, Israel has a positive and negative side to its ledger. And as with any other nation, some people will tend to judge it kindlier than others. Yet unlike other nations, it is targeted with exceptional levels of hatred.

The old one-two

Antisemitism has always followed the same two basic steps. With Jews existing within Christian or Muslim societies on sufferance, the determination to destroy them naturally followed their demonisation. The Nazi regime, for example, spent years building up hostility towards Jews via propaganda that blamed them for all the ills of the world. This laid the groundwork for the Final Solution.

First demonisation, then destruction. But within these two steps there has been a great deal of variety, as antisemitism has kept pace with prevailing trends. In 1791, at the end of the French Revolution, Jews in France were granted full citizenship and equality. This was the first time in history that they had been emancipated, leaving behind the medieval bigotry that subjected the Christ-killers to blood libels, expulsion and murder. Characteristically, the old parasite adapted to the new host, and by the nineteenth century, as the rise of the Rothschild dynasty led to conspiracy theories about the hidden hand of Jewish power, the Jews were being blamed for the corruption of the new liberal world, with its newspapers, stock markets and modern wars.

This was seen in 1894, when the Jewish French army officer Alfred Dreyfus was accused of betraying secrets about artillery technology to the Germans, and convicted as a traitor in a secret court martial. The disgrace of Dreyfus was staged as a public spectacle. While a crowd jeered, the decorations were cut off his uniform and his sword was broken. Despite the humiliation, he cried out: 'I swear that I am innocent. I remain worthy of serving in the army. Long live France! Long live the army!' The unfortunate officer was sent to the penal colony on Devil's Island in French Guiana in South America. Of course, the Jewish officer was indeed innocent. The real culprit was another soldier called Ferdinand Walsin Esterhazy, who admitted it.[78] The novelist Zola exposed the outrage in '*J'accuse*', an open letter to the president, for which he was found guilty of libel; he may have been asphyxiated in retaliation.

Shamefully, although this miscarriage of justice became known to the French top brass, they covered it up for as long as they could. Dreyfus was eventually exonerated only seven years later, after a public outcry. The case dominated the news and divided France, as it emerged that Dreyfus had been incriminated because he was a Jew, and Jews were seen as traitors.[79] The old antisemitism had been spotted in a different guise. This episode had a profound effect on

Herzl, who covered the story as a journalist and witnessed Parisian mobs howling '*Mort aux Juifs*' in the country that had first emancipated the Jews. 'This reinforced his conviction that assimilation had not only failed but was provoking more antisemitism,' notes Sebag Montefiore. 'He even predicted that antisemitism would one day be legalised in Germany. Herzl concluded that Jews could never be safe without their own homeland.'[80] Yet the father of Zionism died of heart failure in 1904, without seeing the Jewish scapegoat redeemed.

The Dreyfus affair, as it became known, was a notorious example of a trumped-up case leading to a wrongful conviction. Yet it was a modern example of the two-step process of antisemitism: Jews are demonised, evidence of their wickedness fabricated, and the verdict against them, held in the public imagination, is a bigoted one. When it comes to Israelophobia, the same dynamic applies. If Israel is an apartheid regime, why should it have a right to exist? If it is guilty of ethnic cleansing, why shouldn't it be treated as a pariah? If it is behaving like Nazi Germany, doesn't it deserve the same defeat?

In the final decades of the Russian empire, Jew-hatred mutated into a mixture of the old and the new. But the steps of demonisation and destruction could always be discerned. In 1881, when Alexander II was gruesomely assassinated using explosives, the Jews were blamed for murdering God's tsar. Traditional murder and gang-rape were unleashed on the five million Jews across the Russian empire, but it was energised by a more modern conspiracy: Jewish merchants were held responsible for the economic depression. The new emperor, Alexander III, was an especially virulent antisemite. A year after his accession, in 1882, he introduced anti-Jewish laws that triggered further waves of persecution and pogroms. The momentum was maintained by his equally bigoted son, Nicolas II, who took the throne in 1894 and ruled until he was toppled by the Reds. The *Protocols of the Elders of Zion* first appeared during his reign, serialised in the ultra-nationalist *Znamya* newspaper; in 1917, during his house arrest at the hands of revolutionaries, Nicolas read the antisemitic forgery aloud to his family. This period changed Russian Jewry forever. Many became Bolsheviks, while millions emigrated to the United States and Britain and about forty-five thousand embraced Zionism and flowed into Palestine.

The two step process is an enduring template, but it has been deployed with infinite variety in different societies and different times. The German approach was to adapt existing antisemitic tropes by blending them with a toxic cocktail of pseudo-science, conspiracy theories and superstition.

It began with dehumanisation. In one typical example, from the 1940 propaganda film *The Eternal Jew* (*Der Ewige Jude*), the narrator said: 'Where rats appear, they bring ruin by destroying mankind's goods and foodstuffs. In this way, they spread disease, plague, leprosy, typhoid fever, cholera, dysentery, and so on. They are cunning, cowardly and cruel and are found mostly in large packs. Among the animals, they represent the rudiment of an insidious, underground destruction – just like the Jews among human beings.'[81]

This led to the next conclusion, familiar since medieval

times: the Jewish *Untermenschen* were simultaneously verminous and all-powerful. 'At the beginning of the twentieth century, Jews sit at the junction of the world financial markets,' the film's narrator continued. 'They are an international power. Only one per cent of the world's population, with the help of their capital they terrorise the world stock exchanges, world opinion, and world politics.'[82] As Hitler himself put it, the goal was supposedly 'the enslavement of German labour power to Jewish finance'.[83] One common Jewish joke from the period, recounted in 2008 by the writer Christopher Hitchens, imagines an oppressed Jewish man reading the Nazi propaganda paper, *Der Stürmer*. When asked why, he explained: 'I read *Der Stürmer*, and there's finally some good news. It seems that we Jews own and control the whole world!'[84]

How did these *Übermenschen-Untermenschen* supposedly use their might? For the destruction of Germany and all that was good. This was demonisation's next move. A slogan that accompanied the *Der Stürmer* editorial read: '*Die Juden sind unser Unglück*', or 'the Jews are our misfortune'.[85] Extending from this, a common Nazi trope blamed the Jews for the Second World War. A vivid propaganda poster from 1942 showed a sinister Jew lurking behind the flags of Britain, the United States and the Soviet Union, accompanied by the words, '*Hinter den Feindmächten: der Jude*', or 'behind the enemy powers: the Jew'.[86] (This idea left an indelible impression. In 2006, the actor Mel Gibson told a policeman arresting him for drunk driving: 'Fucking Jews. The Jews are responsible for all the wars in the world.')[87]

The German public had been softened up for the final step. After years of demonisation, they were ready to accept the 'annihilation of the Jewish race in Europe', as Hitler infamously put it.[88] In 1941, Joseph Goebbels was able to write in an article: 'The Jews are meeting with a fate that may be harsh but is also more than deserved. In this case, pity or regret is completely inappropriate.'[89] Few people turned a hair. How else were decent Aryans expected to deal with such a dangerous and malignant race in their midst?

The octopus lobby

These mechanisms of racial and religious antisemitism have been transferred largely intact into the political vehicle of Israelophobia. The same basic narrative stands: Israel is evil so it must be eradicated. Demonisation demands destruction. Echoing not only twentieth century antisemitism but that of the medieval blood libel – which began in England in 1144 and spread throughout Europe, Russia and the Middle East – contemporary Israelis are accused of murdering Palestinian children to sell their organs for profit and are dehumanised as 'descendants of apes and pigs' in mosque sermons and school textbooks.[90] The myth of Judas and his thirty pieces of silver became the Jewish moneylender, which became the Jewish banker controlling world finances, which has become the Zionists buying up politicians. The greedy Jew has become the Israeli, with his troubling taste for other people's land. The depiction of Jews with horns, cloven hoofs and tails, popular in eleventh-century Christendom, is mirrored in the portrayal of Israelis as Nazis, the modern devils. The old tropes are so deeply embedded in so many cultures that Israelophobia has seamlessly absorbed them.

Among the many Israelophobic cartoons that circulate online is a depiction of an octopus Israel clamped over the Capitol Building or the Statue of Liberty. This is clearly derived from a Nazi cartoon that portrayed the Jew as an octopus with the world in its grip. Similarly, the way that today's Israelophobes talk of the 'Zionist lobby' that holds western governments in the palm of its hand has obvious antecedents in Nazi rhetoric, which alleged shadowy Jewish control of international finance and politics. After Jeremy Corbyn's thumping defeat in 2019, the hard-left former Labour MP Chris Williamson concluded: 'A hostile foreign government has mobilised its assets in the UK – which Israeli diplomats call their "power multiplier" – in an attempt to prevent a

Corbyn-led Labour government from being elected'.[91]

The conspiratorial ravings of Israelophobia are often distinguishable from older antisemitism only by the introduction of the word 'Zionist'. The left-wing sociology professor David Miller, who was sacked from Bristol University in 2021, showed his students diagrams of Jewish groups in Britain, claiming they formed a network of 'Zionist' control. He described the Community Security Trust, for example, a charity providing security guards for synagogues and schools, as 'an organisation that exists to run point for a hostile foreign government in the UK,' adding: 'this is a straightforward story of influence peddling by a foreign state.'[92]

When Miller was sacked, he was not chastened. His demise was the result of 'a pressure campaign against me overseen and directed by a hostile foreign government', he ranted, and 'Israel's assets in the UK' had been 'emboldened by the University collaborating with them to shut down teaching about Islamophobia'. In a parting shot, Miller said: 'The University of Bristol is no longer safe for Muslim, Arab or Palestinian students.'[93] He went on to become a pundit on Iranian state television, where Jeremy Corbyn has also appeared.[94]

As ever, the briefest consideration of the evidence reveals demonisation at work. Take the 'Zionist lobby'. Israel does have lobbyists, of course, but so do hundreds of other countries, corporations and interest groups, many of whom outspend the Jewish state. According to the OpenSecrets list[95] of the top ten biggest spending foreign lobbies in the United States over the past three years, Israel is not present. You must stretch the timeline several years into the past before it appears. And then only just. Looking at the data between 2016 and 2022, top of the list is China, spending an astonishing US$293 million. In second place comes Japan, then South Korea, then Qatar and the Marshall Islands in the Pacific, which shelled out US$214 million. At number six is United Arab Emirates, dropping US$175 million, followed by Russia at number seven. Israel comes in eighth, parting with $162 million, mainly due to a spike in expenditure in 2017 and 2018. The final two places are occupied by Saudi Arabia and Ireland, spending US$159 million and US$139 million respectively. Anybody who has spent time in political circles will have encountered an array of lobbyists. One well-known peer tries to elegantly push the interests of a particular oil-rich Arab state every time I bump into him. But only in the case of Israel is this seen as a sinister conspiracy.

In another striking parallel, the demonisation of the Jews

as being responsible for the world's wars – seen not just in Nazi rhetoric but in the earlier *Protocols of the Elders of Zion* and the French and German antisemitic literature on which it was based – has also been translated into the lexicon of Israelophobia. One recent narrative has it that the Zionists were behind the war in Ukraine in an attempt to prompt Jews to emigrate to Israel; in multiple tweets, anti-Israel activist Susan Abulhawa referred to Ukrainians fleeing to the Jewish state as 'white supremacist colonisers'.[96]

With the demonisation trope firmly established that Israel is controlling world governments, stealing the organs of Palestinian children, practising apartheid and genocide, and fuelling the war in Ukraine, it is not difficult to gain support for its eradication. As it is the twenty-first century, however, these solutions are couched in the language of social justice. The popular chant 'from the river to the sea, Palestine will be free', which appears to be a slogan of resistance and liberation, contains a demand for the obliteration of Israel, which is located between the Jordan river and the Mediterranean Sea. And calls for a 'one state solution' – which on the surface appear equitable – are used as code for the erasure of the Jewish state.

In this postwar age, the time when people in the west could call for the liquidation of the Jews has passed. But it is perfectly acceptable to use the current argot, in which demonised Israel faces self-righteous demands for its destruction. It has become so acceptable, in fact, that it never even occurs to those who indulge in this rhetoric to wonder why no other country in the world stands accused of having 'no right to exist'.

Chapter Four

WEAPONISATION
THE SECOND CHARACTERISTIC OF ISRAELOPHOBIA

Using the social justice movement as a Trojan horse for hatred of Jews and their national home

By the left

Antisemitism has always had the ability to use a society's dominant beliefs, whether religious or secular, as a Trojan horse to attack the Jews. Communism provided an opportunity to cast them as the agents of international capitalism, while capitalism allowed people to disparage them as communists. Christianity inspired countless pogroms over the centuries, from the Lisbon Massacre of 1506 – in which up to four thousand Jews were butchered and their bodies burnt in the church square – to the 1946 lynching of Holocaust survivors in Hungary and Poland, in the false belief that they had been turning Christian children into matzo and sausages.[1] Jews have been killed in the name of Islam many times throughout history, from the Grenada massacre of 1066 to the Islamist atrocities of today. The advance of science in the twentieth century allowed that too to be weaponised, with Nazi doctors measuring Jews' noses and heads with callipers to 'prove' they were an inferior race and conducting gruesome experiments on Jewish twins at Auschwitz.

The Holocaust, the most horrifying example of anti-Jewish racism in recent history, discredited Nazi-style antisemitism in the west. So, with religion in decline, the hatred moved on once more, this time adopting the language and tropes of identity politics and harnessing the energy of the social justice cause. Israel has become the primary target of the fashionable anti-colonialist, anti-imperialist and anti-racist movement, even though the creation of the Jewish state was neither colonialist, imperialist nor racist. By framing it in this way, the new antisemites can pose as the good guys, insisting that the right is the only home of racism. As the academic David Hirsh wrote: 'Today's antisemitism is difficult to recognise because it does not come dressed in a Nazi uniform and it does not openly proclaim its hatred or fear of Jews. In fact, it says it has learnt the lessons of Jew-hatred better than most Jews have, and it says that, unlike them, it stands in the anti-racist tradition. It is an antisemitism which positions Jews themselves as "oppressors", and it positions those who develop hostile narratives about Jews as "oppressed".'[2]

It is these ideological acrobatics that allowed Jeremy Corbyn to sign the book of remembrance for Holocaust Memorial Day in 2017,[3] even though he had supported a motion for it to be renamed 'Genocide Memorial Day',[4] had hosted a Holocaust memorial event at which Israel was compared to the Nazis[5] and had called Hamas and Hezbollah, the modern Jew-killers, his 'friends'.[6] As Baudelaire put it, 'the greatest trick the Devil ever pulled was convincing the world he didn't exist'.[7]

None of this means that the old-fashioned antisemitism has vanished, of course. In many shadowy corners, unreconstructed strains of the virus continue to thrive. In places like France, Germany and the United States, where right-wing populism is a significant force, anti-Jewish bigotry can be found embedded in the conservative side of the political divide. Dark things crawl through movements like QAnon and the Proud Boys; the 2018 Tree of Life synagogue shooting in Pittsburgh gave an example – as if one more was needed – of how such prejudice can still turn deadly.[8] Even older forms of Jew-hatred can still be seen. In January 2023, the disgraced Catholic bishop Richard Nelson Williamson gave an interview to Iranian television using language that could have come straight out of the Middle Ages. 'The Jews are given power by the devil,' he said. 'Almighty God allows them to do what they do, but it is the devil who shows them how to take power and government control.'[9]

These forms of antisemitism are easier to spot, however, as they are allied to the more familiar language of religious hatred, xenophobia and hyper-nationalism (whoever invented the American white supremacist chant 'Jews will not replace us' didn't even bother reaching for the word 'Zionists')[10]. On the more self-conscious left, by contrast, antisemitism tends to require the cover of Israelophobia. This mutation is spreading far quicker than older variants.

Even some far-right firebrands, already well conversant in tropes about greedy Jews controlling the media and international finance, are starting to take cover in this lexicon. In June 2023, photographs circulated of members of the 'Goyim Defence League', an American neo-Nazi group, dressing up in Third Reich helmets and camouflage fatigues and performing the Hitler salute while they burnt and shot at an Israeli flag. The new pathology is subsuming older versions in every strand of society.

Even Jews, particularly those on the left, can find it difficult to identify antisemitism when it cloaks itself in bien pensant rhetoric about Israel. As the former *New York Times* journalist Bari Weiss – whose childhood synagogue was the Tree of Life – puts it: 'American Jews tend to be much more attuned to antisemitism when it comes from the political right. Certainly, this is a function of Hitler's long shadow. But it is also because American Jews have a deep affinity with the political left.'[11]

Left right left

The synergy between the progressive movement and antisemitism goes back a long way. Indeed, it has been happening since the very beginning, as can be seen in the life of the English satirical pamphleteer, chronicler and politician William Cobbett, one of the earliest left-wingers.

Born in Surrey in 1763, Cobbett became a celebrated champion of the poor, whose book, *Rural Rides*, has never been out of print. Ideologically idiosyncratic, he was a staunch defender of the underdog, campaigning for the franchise to be broadened and lobbying for workers' rights at the height of the Industrial Revolution. He became a hero of later leftist intellectuals, including Karl Marx and Michael Foot. It goes without saying that Cobbett and Jeremy Corbyn would have got on. The former's basic worldview was that if only the corrupt politicians, fund-holders, commercial interests, East India merchants and political economists could be swept away, England would once again be serene and happy. Two centuries later, Corbyn criticised the 'tax dodgers, dodgy landlords, bad bosses and big polluters',[12] and questioned the hankering after constant economic growth.

If, as Sir Isaiah Berlin supposedly said, an antisemite is someone who hates the Jews more than absolutely necessary, then in addition to being a brilliant journalist and campaigner – and in spite of the biographies that wilfully ignore the fact, seeing him only as the 'poor man's friend'[13] – Cobbett was a swivel-eyed antisemite (he also hated blacks, Scots and most foreigners). This nineteenth century champion of the downtrodden personified the blurring of medieval antisemitism with conspiracy theories that aligned Jews with the hidden forces of finance, an idea that to this day has a foothold in the progressive movement. As if that wasn't enough, his beliefs also aligned with the first stirrings of a new antisemitism that would reach its full expression at Auschwitz in the next century.

Cobbett's prejudice was openly expressed and in the traditional style. 'My dislike of the Jews is that which our forefathers had of them,' he wrote, adding that there was 'something hateful in the very nature of the ceremonies which they have the infamy to call religious'. In 1823, he wrote of his regret that Jews were no longer treated as they had been in former times – banished by Edward I, or at least forced to wear a badge and confined to their homes on Sundays – and he railed against the 'JEW DOG', rendering the slur in capitals.[14] In one particularly venomous moment, he argued that a truly Christian country would 'refuse their burial at all and to cause their carcasses to be flung into the sea'.[15] He went on to defend medieval persecution, proudly relating that in his youth he had pelted Jews with apples and clods of dirt.[16]

His bigotry became more modern, however, when he envisioned Jews as the hidden controllers of finance, the press and society, manipulating workers and noblemen alike to their own ends and pursuing anti-English agendas. For him, sweeping away the fundholders, commercial interests and the rest meant sweeping away the Jews. His belief in 'Jewish predominance' lay behind the single most important passage in all his writing: a conspiratorial article in the 1805 *Political Register* in which he decried a 'system that was ruining the country'.

This system, he ranted, was one of:

> [Upstarts]; of low-bred, low-minded sycophants usurping the stations designed by nature, by reason, by the Constitution, and by the interests of the people, to men of high birth, eminent talents, or great national services; the system by which the ancient Aristocracy and the Church have been undermined; by which the ancient gentry of the kingdom have been almost extinguished, their means of support having

> been transferred, by the hand of the tax gatherer, to contractors, jobbers and Jews.[17]

He later blamed the agricultural crisis on 'Jewish money' in the City of London.[18]

Chillingly, at times Cobbett's attitudes foretold the emergence of a new European antisemitism. 'Nowhere does Cobbett's mood resemble a native reaction as much as in Germany,' the American historian John W. Osborne observed in 1984. 'There, by the late nineteenth century, numerous voices cried hate for the new liberal, materialistic machine civilisation. Antisemitic, rural-based, suspicious of parliaments and political parties, detesting capitalism, cities, and "progress", firm believers in a conspiratorial theory of history, German nationalists tried to destroy the despised present in order to recapture an idealised past.'[19] In the figure of Cobbett, the early left-winger, can be recognised the hallmarks of Hitlerism.

Schrodinger's Jew

Western political culture has morphed in recent decades. Traditionally, conservatives have been preoccupied with individual freedom, lower taxes, a smaller state, immigration and law and order, while progressives have typically focused on fairness, public services, the welfare system, international solidarity and collective bargaining. Now, however, a new set of priorities is in the ascendence on the left. Concerns about race and identity, diversity and inclusion, colonialism, slavery, sexual equality and transgender rights have grown exponentially, particularly among the graduate classes who sit at the top of our institutions. The right, meanwhile, has responded by railing against 'wokism'.

Figured wrongly as a struggle against colonial white supremacists, the Palestinian plight hits the sweet spot in the culture war. In their thirst for a real-life bogeyman, Israelophobes craft a Jewish nemesis; the cause has grown so potent that it is now an entry card into liberal society. It is hard to imagine friends of Israel being truly welcomed by progressives, even if they happen to be dyed-in-the-wool socialists.

If this was only about concern for the Palestinians, when the Assad regime dropped barrel bombs on a Palestinian refugee camps in south-eastern Syria, or when Hamas subjected its own citizens in Gaza to 'arbitrary detention, torture and other ill-treatment, and use of excessive force against protesters' (as Amnesty International put it),[20] there would have been howls of protest. When Israel attacked terrorist strongholds in Gaza, tens of thousands rallied in London and New York; when Assad attacked Palestinian communities in Yarmouk, nothing. The frequent atrocities that take place elsewhere in the Islamic world, from Yemen to Iraq, rarely attract attention. It is hard to avoid the conclusion that progressives aren't too outraged about dead Muslims unless Jews are doing the killing.

In the new world of identity politics, victimhood is seen through an ideological prism. The underdog will be championed with boundless energy, but only if it is the right underdog. There's no point wasting energy at a rally for Tigrayans, for instance, because both aggressors and victims are Ethiopians, so it isn't going to advance the struggle against structural racism; and there's certainly no point lamenting murdered Israelis when they are crudely categorised as white. This helps explain why the Palestinian plight has achieved such totemic status, while other injustices – from the Rohingya genocide to the persecution of democratic activists in Iran – pass almost unnoticed. Campaigning against the Burmese, Iranian, Chinese or North Korean regimes has limited value in the culture wars. In other words, it's not about the Palestinians, it's about the perpetrators. It's about the supposedly powerful and privileged. It's about the Jews.

A video of a pro-Palestinian rally in Britain sums this up. Speaking laboriously through a megaphone, a woman of late middle-age declares: 'In Manchester, we have a banner saying, "Manchester supports the resistance". And there's only one solution: intifada revolution. And quite often, activists shy away from that. We worry about Palestinians taking actions of violence . . . [But] there's no peaceful solution as far as Israel's concerned.'[21]

The two intifadas, or uprisings, claimed thousands of innocent lives, as Palestinian militants carried out waves of bombings, rocket attacks and shootings of civilians, while Israel conducted counter-terror operations with infantry, tanks and aerial assaults. The first created a power vacuum that in 1987 brought forth the jihadist group Hamas, a branch of the Egyptian Muslim Brotherhood, which was dedicated to Israel's destruction. It drove a wedge between Jews and Arabs, who no longer worked together or walked through each other's neighbourhoods.

The second, with its string of sickening suicide attacks on Israeli buses, destroyed trust in the peace process, caused the country to lurch to the right and precipitated a schism in the Palestinian camp.

Yet while ordinary people living in the region pray for peace, a woman in Manchester calls for the murder of Jews and a new spiral of violence. It is the equivalent of activists in Boston demanding another IRA bombing campaign in London and the dismantlement of the Good Friday Agreement. It was no coincidence that the organisation that the speaker supported, the Palestinian Solidarity Campaign, is affiliated to fifteen of Britain's largest trade unions.[22] Clearly, this was less about compassion for Palestinian lives than the expression of ideology.

All about that race

Take a step back and the situation on the contemporary left looks woeful. From Jeremy Corbyn's infamous remark that British 'Zionists' don't understand 'English irony' – one of the most consequential stories I've broken as a journalist – to US congresswoman Ilhan Omar's claim that Israel had 'hypnotised' the world not to see its 'evildoings', as if it had some medieval Jewish mystical power, to left-wing Spanish politician Pablo Iglesias Turrión's discussions about the power of the 'pro-Israel lobby' on an Iranian-funded talk show,[23] to Greek trade unionists sticking pictures of dead Palestinians to the Holocaust monument in Thessaloniki, and a thousand other examples, the bigotry often bears the fingerprints of progressives. This sort of prejudice overlaps with the hatred that is rife in the Muslim world. In an example of the horseshoe of politics, it also sometimes overlaps with the far-right; at the height of the Labour antisemitism controversy, the former British National Party leader Nick Griffin backed Jeremy Corbyn.[24]

Largely, this stems from the influx of radical racial ideology into progressive circles. At the beginning of the civil rights movement, the Jewish community stood shoulder-to-shoulder with Martin Luther King. As a result, synagogues were attacked by the Ku Klux Klan. *Strange Fruit*, Billie Holiday's iconic protest song about a lynching in Indiana, was written by Abel Meeropol, a Jewish high school teacher. In Britain, the British Jewish tennis player Angela Buxton partnered with the African-American star Althea Gibson in 1956 to face down racism and win the women's doubles title at Wimbledon. This affinity also had a Zionist dimension. Golda Meir, Israel's first female leader, pointed out in her memoir that 'we Jews share with the African peoples a memory of centuries-long suffering'. She recalled that many years before, Herzl himself had vowed: 'Once I have witnessed the redemption of the Jews, my people, I wish also to assist in the redemption of the Africans.'[25]

The solidarity was reciprocal. In 1966, Martin Luther King demanded justice for persecuted Jews behind the Iron Curtain. 'The absence of opportunity to associate as Jews in the enjoyment of Jewish culture and religious experience becomes a severe limitation upon the individual,' he said. 'Negros can well understand and sympathise with this problem.' In typically uncompromising style, he added that Jewish history and culture were 'part of everyone's heritage, whether he be Jewish, Christian or Moslem'. He concluded: 'We cannot sit complacently by the wayside while our Jewish brothers in the Soviet Union face the possible extinction of their cultural and spiritual life. Those that sit at rest, while others take pains, are tender turtles, and buy their quiet with disgrace.'[26]

Once the militant Malcolm X replaced Martin Luther King as the dominant figure in the black liberation movement, however, this solidarity became strained. Malcolm X tended to associate the Jews with power and often veered into antisemitism. Throughout his life, he attacked what he called 'Zionist-Dollarism', deplored Israel and cast Jews as a race of white oppressors. In his autobiography – which contains examples of the crudest bigotry – he poured scorn on the bond between Jews and the civil rights movement. 'So many Jews actually were hypocrites in their claim to be friends of the American black man,' he wrote. 'I gave the Jew credit for being among all other whites the most active, and the most vocal, financial, "leader" and "liberal" in the Negro civil rights movement. But at the same time, I knew that the Jew played these roles for a very careful strategic reason: the more prejudice in America could be focused upon the Negro, then the more the white Gentiles' prejudice would keep diverted off the Jew.'[27]

Fast-forward to the present, and the radical racial ideas of 1960s and 1970s America have evolved into an all-consuming political ideology that has spread across the west. Because Critical Race Theory, the philosophy behind the social justice movement, holds that 'racism equals prejudice plus power'[28] – a notion introduced in 1970 by the American psychologist Patricia Bidol-Padva – it teaches that whites cannot experience racism. A hierarchy of grievance has sprung up with blacks at the pinnacle. Non-black minorities like Armenians, Roma or Jews are explicitly barred from victimhood, even when they are targeted more than blacks. And with centuries of ingrained antisemitism latching onto Israel, devotees of identity politics are unable to help themselves shoehorning Jewish people, who within living memory were murdered in their millions because of their race, into the category of white oppressor. Whoopi Goldberg pursued that logic to its absurd conclusion in 2022, when she found herself arguing on television that the Holocaust was 'not about race',[29] as it involved 'two groups of white people', even though Nazi ideology explicitly defined Jews as racially inferior.

Similarly, in April 2023, the British MP Diane Abbott was suspended from the Labour Party after writing to the *Observer* newspaper claiming that Jews could not face racism, as they were only 'white people with points of difference, such as redheads'. It is comforting that she was censured so quickly. But the ease with which she ignored two millennia of antisemitism, appearing to forget even the Holocaust, and the lack of hesitation on the part of the left-wing *Observer* in publishing these claims, demonstrates how ideology often feels like reality on the left. It also demonstrates how pervasive American identity politics has become in Britain and across the western world.

The political chant of a generation

At the peak of his political career, more than two-thirds of British university students supported Jeremy Corbyn.[30] Several years have passed since the old socialist was rejected by the rest of the British electorate at the ballot box. But the legacy of the cultural shift that he epitomised can still be seen today. He was elected Labour leader as a dinosaur of the old left, who had come of age during the Cold War amidst the CND movement and fringe Marxist activism. For years, he was a columnist for the *Morning Star* newspaper, which is aligned with the manifesto of the Communist Party of Britain; he also had connections at the related title *Soviet Weekly*, the propaganda paper published by Sovinformburo, the USSR's news agency, from the Soviet Embassy in London. His politics remained static all his adult life. Yet his political base was Britain's ultra-progressive, digitally native youth. Corbyn's campaigning was a blend of old-fashioned rallies and his supporters' savvy online activism, and for several years it worked: in 2017, a radical 'youthquake' erupted when he appeared on stage at the Wirral Live rock festival to shouts of 'Oh, Jeremy Corbyn' by thousands of youngsters, most of them a third of his age. The *Guardian* described it glowingly as 'the political chant of a generation'.[31] But both the older and younger generations of the movement were shot through with Israelophobia.

This phenomenon was mirrored on the other side of the Atlantic in the figure of Bernie Sanders, who describes himself as a 'democratic socialist' and ran for the presidential nomination on a radical platform of left-wing reform.

During the 2020 race, he commanded the support of a majority of Democrats under thirty, who had no memory of the Cold War but felt sharply the effects of the 2008 financial crash.[32] Sanders, who 'stood in solidarity' with Corbyn in 2019, has attracted a cloud of Israelophobia concerns himself, due largely to the outspoken characters in his team.[33] His own position on Israel is far to the left of mainstream Democrats; he said he would make American military aid to the country conditional on its behaviour and has attacked Benjamin Netanyahu as a 'racist'.[34]

Sanders' legacy is nurtured by activists like Linda Sarsour, a radical anti-Zionist who supports boycotting the Jewish state, and 'the Squad', a group of young, far-left Democratic politicians united by charisma, progressive principles and a disgust for Israel. Corbyn and Sanders may be receding from the political stage, but the blend of traditional socialism and identity politics that buoyed them on a digitally driven tidal wave hasn't gone away. The common denominator is victimhood; whereas old-fashioned Marxists see society as a struggle between powerful capitalists and oppressed workers, young devotees of identity politics see a struggle between privileged races and powerless minorities. In Israel, both generations project everything they loathe.

It is telling that the people who seethe most against the Middle East's only democracy tend to harbour sympathies for the autocracies of Russia, Iran and the murderous regime in Damascus, all of which have brought far more death and destruction to the world. Corbyn has been repeatedly branded Putin's 'useful idiot' for taking a soft stance on Russian assassination attempts, opposing Nato[35] and speaking at a Russian propaganda event in New York while Putin's troops attacked Ukraine.[36] He has attended celebrations to mark the brutal Iranian revolution, lamented the theocracy's 'demonisation' and appeared frequently on Iranian state television.[37] In Syria, the 2011 civil war killed up to 600,000 people,[38] of whom 307,000 were civilians, according to figures released in March 2023;[39] the US-led invasion of Iraq caused 601,000 violent deaths between 2003 and 2006 alone. By comparison, statistics from 2021 showed that in the entire seventy-five years of Israel's history, the sum total of combat deaths on both sides amounted to about 86,000.[40] Yet the outrage of Corbyn and his fellow travellers in the United States and across the west has been largely directed at the Jewish state. It has even become commonplace for the sole democracy in the Middle East, which has a notable absence of death camps, to be compared to Hitler's Third Reich.

This is just one of the egregious slurs directed by many on the left at the Jewish state. It is transparently false. There is much injustice and conflict in Israel's story, to be sure, but the Palestinian population has grown from under a million in 1948 to more than five million today. Any Israeli attempt at a genocide would have been pretty inept. Those who make the allegation are strangely oblivious to the insult to the victims of Rwanda, Darfur, Bosnia, Cambodia and of course the Holocaust. In a crowded field, accusing Jews of committing the very crimes they have suffered is one of the least savoury habits of Israelophobia. But the strategic value of the comparison is obvious. That Nazism was an evil is one of the last things that almost everybody in the west agrees upon, with the Holocaust presenting one of very few crimes that all branches of politics condemn. Not only does lumping Israel into the same category as the Third Reich imply that the two regimes deserve the same fate, but it offers a frisson of poetic justice in the idea that the Jews have morphed into their oppressors. Cartoons abound in which Israelis are gleefully depicted as Nazis. Some Israelophobes, intoxicated by their own rhetoric, even manage to downplay or deny the Holocaust while accusing the Jews of perpetrating it upon the Arabs.

The claims can become even more unhinged than that. Guests on BBC programmes have stated that the Jewish state has no culture of its own apart from what it 'takes from the original peoples'.[41] Mossad has been accused of infiltrating a shark into the Red Sea that ate a German grandmother.[42] During the late Queen's jubilee, a council in Nelson, Lancashire – an old mill town with a population of twenty-nine thousand, more than three thousand miles from Jerusalem – flew the Palestinian flag instead of the Union Jack.[43] No other democracy is targeted in this way. And no dictatorship either.

Despite all this, Israel's left-wing detractors often claim that accusations of antisemitism are only used to silence pro-Palestinian dissent. Some argue that Corbyn – who wrote a glowing foreword to a book that argued that European finance was controlled by 'men of a single and peculiar race'[44] – was the victim of a smear campaign because he dared to speak up for the underdog. As the novelist Howard Jacobson retorted: 'Those who say we shouldn't conflate anti-Zionism and antisemitism should give up employing the language of medieval Jew-hatred to vilify Israel.'[45]

Titanic fail

In 2022, *Eleven Days in May*, a film about the previous year's Gaza conflict was released. Narrated by Kate Winslet, it examined the deaths of sixty Palestinian young people in a highly emotive manner, while turning a blind eye to the threat to Israel. Before long, people began noticing inaccuracies. In the script, Winslet suggested that Israel had 'loaded up its fighter jets' with bombs and missiles after 'plastic bottles' were thrown at security forces in Jerusalem and just seven rockets were launched from Gaza. In truth, Israel had taken military action against Hamas targets after seventy-six rockets had been launched indiscriminately at its civilian populations; the documentary made no mention of the 4,360 rockets fired at Israel during the ensuing conflict, or the thirteen Israelis who had lost their lives. Moreover, seven of the dead Palestinian youngsters featured in the film had actually perished when Hamas' own rockets mistakenly hit Gaza, while several others were underage combatants, killed while mounting attacks alongside adult militants. The whole thing began to resemble a stitch-up.[46]

How could this have happened? There were clues. The distinguished British director, Michael Winterbottom, had not travelled to the region for the making of the film. Instead, he had relied on Mohammed Sawwaf, a Gazan, for on-the-ground material. Here, the plot thickened. On social media, Sawwaf – who was billed as co-director – had celebrated the launching of rockets at civilian targets and stated that the map of Palestine should extend 'from the sea to the river', code for the dismantlement of Israel. More damningly, it turned out that Hamas had granted him an award for 'countering the Zionist narrative'. Was there any wonder that the film was not entirely impartial?

Which brings us to another question. How did Winslet – and Winterbottom, for that matter – become weaponised by this apparent propaganda project? When the controversy erupted, the actress pleaded ignorance. 'That my participation could be interpreted as taking a stand on the rights and wrongs of one of the world's most tragic and intractable conflicts never entered my thinking,' she said. 'War is a tragedy for all sides. Children have no voice in conflict. I simply wanted to lend them mine.'[47] There is no reason to doubt the actress' intentions, or indeed her naïveté. Presumably, the one-sided film didn't sound any alarm bells in her head, even as she narrated its obvious untruths in a recording studio. It didn't, presumably, feel wrong to her. Indeed, it seems likely that it felt right.

Winslet is far from the only progressive to have been unwittingly weaponised by the Hamas agenda. At the height of the same conflict in 2021, the *New York Times*, America's left-wing paper of record, published a searing front page mourning sixty-four young Palestinian victims. (It had denied this treatment to the many civilian casualties of the vicious Turkish assault on the Kurds, or the Royal Air Force's 'major air offensive' in Iraq, both of which occurred at around the same time.) Under a headline reminding us that 'They Were Just Children', the page was dominated by a poignant grid of young faces. In the article, the Gray Lady, as the venerable paper is known, informed readers that 'they had wanted to be doctors, artists and leaders'. Yet once again, inaccuracies had crept in. It soon emerged that, as was the case with the Winslet film, at least ten of the *New York Times*'s casualties had been killed by Hamas' own rockets falling short in Gaza, while at least two had been participating in attacks. As if this wasn't enough, the paper had even included a photograph from six years before of an unidentified girl wrapped in a keffiyeh, which it wrongly presented as one of the dead.[48] Seemingly, their enthralment to the Israelophobic narrative caused the US's most respected editors to take leave of their basic journalistic standards.

There have been many other instances of this. One landmark came in 2002. After thirty Jewish civilians were murdered in a suicide attack on a Netanya hotel during Passover, Israeli forces targeted terrorists in the West Bank city of Jenin and a bloody battle ensued. The British press overflowed with outrage. 'A monstrous war crime that Israel has tried to cover up for a fortnight has finally been exposed,' howled the *Independent*. Its correspondent, Phil Reeves, based his report on the testimony of a lone eyewitness, Kamal Anis, who reported seeing Israeli soldiers 'pile thirty bodies beneath a half-wrecked house. When the pile was complete, they bulldozed the building, bringing its ruins down on the corpses. Then they flattened the area with a tank'. The *Daily Telegraph* ran the same story. The *Guardian* published an emotive leading article comparing the operation in Jenin – which had left fifty-three Palestinians and twenty-three Israelis dead – to the 9/11 atrocities, which had killed almost three thousand. The correspondent for the *Times of London*, Janine di Giovanni, was equally scathing. 'Rarely in more than a decade of war reporting . . . have I seen such deliberate destruction, such disrespect for human life,' she wrote. But neither she nor anybody else can have seen it. The 'deliberate destruction' had not taken place. No adequate apologies were ever offered.[49]

Hamas in the media

In the age of social media, fake news flies in all directions all the time. On Italian Facebook, a viral picture of a toddler suffering from Sturge-Weber syndrome, a rare and painful skin condition, was wrongly labelled as evidence of Israeli brutality,[50] while Twitter footage of Palestinians applying artificial blood and make-up for a medical training programme was wrongly passed off as evidence of an elaborate attempt to dupe the media.[51] But Facebook and Twitter are not the *New York Times*, the *Times of London* or the *Daily Telegraph*; anonymous accounts are not Kate Winslet.

It's not just the world's foremost liberal paper and one of the world's most recognisable actresses that are weaponised. Supermodel Bella Hadid claimed that 'Israel invaded a Palestinian refugee camp and massacred nine people, including an elderly woman,' when in truth the incursion was a counter-terror operation and seven of the dead were Hamas and Islamic Jihad gunmen.[52] And who can forget the BBC headline, 'Palestinian shot dead after Jerusalem attack kills two', as if the main outrage was that the Israeli police shot the rampaging double murderer?[53] The fact that Israelophobic propaganda can exert so much influence, even over the supposedly even-handed BBC, speaks volumes about its pervasiveness. Sometimes it is subtle, sometimes less subtle, but all too often it is there. Few, if any, of these journalists and celebrities will have been intentionally biased. But under the weight of their own assumptions, when they fail to uphold impartiality, they tend to fail in the same direction.

To a person infected by Israelophobia, positive news about the place feels worthy of the highest suspicion. A brief scroll through *Guardian* stories about the Jewish state will prove that they are overwhelmingly negative, much more so than those about other countries. Israel can't do anything, it seems, without being accused by activists of 'whitewashing' the conflict. Hosting a cycling race is 'sportswashing';[54] promoting environmental causes and diets is 'greenwashing'[55] or 'veganwashing';[56] staging a Pride rally is 'pinkwashing';[57] promoting women's rights is 'purplewashing';[58] even producing wine is 'winewashing'.[59] If they can't hold sports events, support gay and women's rights, care about the planet, eat vegan food or make wine, what are Israelis supposed to do with their time? If you Google the list of different types of 'washing', hatred radiates from the screen. In the Israelophobic imagination, the country is only allowed to exist as an oppressive, apartheid autocracy, not a real and complex place with its own history and culture, its own sports and cuisine, its own morality and immorality, its own light and its own shade.

Once again, Israelophobia is a recognisable repackaging of old-fashioned antisemitism. This disgust towards Jews simply living their lives has been commonplace for centuries. 'The Jew, [an antisemite] says, is completely bad, completely a Jew,' wrote the existentialist philosopher Jean-Paul Sartre in 1948.

> His virtues, if he has any, turn to vices by reason of the fact that they are his; work coming from his hands necessarily bears his stigma. If he builds a bridge, that bridge, being Jewish, is bad from the first to the last span. The same action carried out by a Jew and by a Christian does not have the same meaning in the two cases, for the Jew contaminates all that he touches with an I-know-not-what execrable quality . . . Strictly speaking, the Jew contaminates even the air he breathes.[60]

Observing all this, terrorist groups attempt to lure liberals into furthering their cause by using the language and themes of the social justice movement as a further Trojan horse. In January, Deutsche Welle, Germany's centre-left, state funded broadcaster, was forced to apologise after airing an interview with Hazem Qassem, a spokesman for Hamas, as if he was a respectable commentator.[61] At the time, the Israeli leader Benjamin Netanyahu had just formed a coalition government that included several religious chauvinists and far-right ideologues, causing consternation both in Israel and in Jewish communities worldwide. The Hamas spokesman exploited this febrility. Israel's new government was, he told millions of German viewers, 'terrorist, fascist, racist like never before'. So now Hamas cares about terrorism, fascism and racism? The irony was breath-taking. For an official from a repressive Islamist regime to weaponise liberal buzzwords to smear a democracy was the very epitome of chutzpah. It was even more astounding to see the terrorist spokesman taken seriously by Germany's state broadcaster. Here, in real-time, was the cross-fertilisation between western liberals and Islamist fanatics.

The unedifying spectacle of western progressives allying with the most fanatical, racist Islamist groups on Earth has become a feature of the hard-left. One need look no further than Corbyn, who attended a wreath-laying ceremony for dead terrorists. In any other circumstances, regimes that enforce Sharia, carry out shootings and suicide attacks, execute homosexuals and imprison and torture their own citizens would be condemned outright by the left. But not when they stand against Jews.

All white

History shows that Israel does not conform to the paradigm of the Caucasian imperialist oppressor that is so hated by progressive activists. It is true that its founding fathers lived at a time when colonialism was accepted, and many shared certain paternalistic attitudes with British and European empire builders, but the similarities only go so far. Britain had no ancestral claim on India, for example. The British were not a persecuted diaspora people who had been rounded up, worked to death, shot, gassed and subjected to pseudo-medical experiments in the worst genocide the world had seen. Britons had not been languishing in foreign lands for two thousand years, preserving their culture and longing for a return to their homeland. British empire builders did not intend to share the land with its other inhabitants, as the Zionists did, but to rule them. And British colonial crimes, both in scale and in vindictiveness, put even the worst behaviour of the rag-tag Jewish pioneers in the shade.

Indeed, Jewish militia who were fighting British mandate troops in Palestine saw themselves as an indigenous people trying to drive out colonial occupiers. It wasn't just the Jews who viewed it that way. In 1946, when a member of the Jewish underground was whipped by the British army – a demeaning colonial punishment – his comrades kidnapped two British officers and subjected them to the same ordeal. This was seen as a source of morale for people living under the yoke of the British Empire all over the world. 'We received congratulations from Irishmen, from Americans, Canadians, Russians, Frenchmen,' Israeli premier Menachem Begin wrote in an account of his time as a militia chief. 'Our brother-Jews throughout the world straightened their backs. After generations of humiliation by whipping, they had witnessed an episode which restored their dignity and self respect. The coloured African and the Chinese coolie, long acquainted with the whip, also raised their heads in joyous acknowledgement.'[62] A French newspaper printed a cartoon of a nervous British soldier holding his helmet over his buttocks.

These days, however, the pickings are thin for a progressive activist in need of a cause. Western empires have collapsed; homosexual relationships are widely accepted in the west; the main battles for sexual and racial equality have been won. Campaigning against microaggressions, misgendering or the particular use of toilets does not make you Rosa Parks, Mahatma Gandhi or Emmeline Pankhurst. However, squint one eye and demonise Israel as a white supremacist, apartheid colonial power, mix in age-old assumptions about Jewish financiers and the Zionist lobby, and you have yourself a cause worth fighting.

Coded antisemitism has always appealed to the left, which seeks to overturn oppressive power structures. In the world of identity politics, however, Jews are not easily placed in the pantheon of race and victimhood. Jewishness, which is passed down through families, has a strong racial component (that much can be established by genetics), but its boundaries are porous, as anybody may join through religious conversion. Are Jews white? At least 20 per cent of them, and about half of those in Israel, are Middle Eastern or north African,[63] and even the ones with Caucasian appearance were seen by the Nazis as the antithesis of Aryan. Are Jews privileged? On the one hand, they suffered one of the world's worst genocides, especially the European Jews who could pass as white; the establishment of Israel led to more Jewish refugees than Palestinian ones; and even in modern Britain, Home Office figures showed that Jews are five times more likely to be targeted by hate crimes than any other group.[64] On the other, Jews in the diaspora – like the Chinese and Indian communities – are often middle class, with a strong family structure and emphasis on education. This leads to relatively greater levels of affluence. Moreover, the antisemitic stereotype of rich, powerful Jews controlling international affairs found a new foothold when Israel went from plucky underdog to regional superpower.

All the above puts race activists into a tailspin, as they cannot pigeonhole Jews as either white or non-white, privileged or oppressed. So they blur their vision and plump for white and privileged. In fact, these days, when whiteness carries negative associations, Jews are often positioned as even whiter than white people, once again giving them a special category of their own. In 2018, Mark Winston Griffith, executive director of the Black Movement Center, a not-for-profit black community group in Crown Heights, New York, suggested that Jewishness was 'a form of almost hyper-whiteness'.[65] Following the two-step mechanism in which demonisation validates destruction, Griffiths added that hyper-whiteness, rather than antisemitism, explained why Jews were being attacked on the streets of Brooklyn.

During the Black Lives Matter (BLM) protests, attempts to cast Jews among the forces of white oppression by spreading the #Jewishprivilege Twitter hashtag were subverted by Jewish people posting accounts of the persecution suffered by their families. But that didn't stop several BLM rallies from descending into rampant Israelophobia and Jew-hatred. As early as 2014, during the unrest that followed the shooting of a black man in Ferguson, Missouri, demonstrators chanted 'from Ferguson to Palestine, occupation is a crime,'[66] and held placards stating, 'Ferguson is Palestine'.[67] In 2020, after the killing of George Floyd, Jewish shops were destroyed, synagogues were sprayed with 'free Palestine' and 'fuck Israel' graffiti, a statue of a Swedish diplomat who had saved Hungarian Jews from the Nazis was defaced with antisemitic slogans,[68] and dark conspiracy theories sprouted about Israelis training the racist American police. In France, a Black Lives Matter rally descended into cries of 'dirty Jews', echoing the antisemitic chants that filled the same streets during the Dreyfus affair a century before.[69] In short, whether

Jews count as non-white, white or hyper-white, privileged or oppressed, colonisers or indigenous has become a matter of Schrodinger's Jew: the label shifts on the basis of the agenda.[70] And when it comes to the social justice movement, that agenda is invariably hostile to their nation-state.

In their time, the Soviets outlawed traditional antisemitism while allowing hatred to run riot in the form of 'anti-Zionism'. Similarly, the final tricksiness of the social justice movement is that it wraps bigotry in political justification, allowing activists to disavow antisemitism while being animated by it. It may be taboo to say Jews should be wiped out, but to demand Palestinian freedom 'from the river to the sea' carries an aura of fashionable virtue. Language matters. In his 1945 essay *Antisemitism in Britain*, Orwell recalled a 'young intellectual, communist or near-communist' remarking: 'No, I do *not* like Jews. I've never made any secret of that. I can't stick them. Mind you, I'm not antisemitic, of course.'[71] Nearly eighty years later, it is striking how little has changed.

Cover me

What has changed, however, is the extent to which Jews on the political margins can be exploited to bolster Israelophobia. In the past, when antisemitism was rooted in race, this was more difficult. It is harder to be an antisemite when you are indelibly the target of the prejudice. With the old bigotry piggybacking on geopolitics, however, Jews find themselves with the option of stepping away from the kill-zone by denouncing Israel. Of course, it never really works; in the final analysis, this is not about the plight of the Palestinians but the Jewishness of the Jewish state. As Jabotinsky put it: 'We are hated not because we are blamed for everything, but we are blamed for everything because we are not loved.'[72] For certain Jewish progressives, however, the Israelification of antisemitism must be a relief. They now have the option of gaining entry into their political milieu by way of auto-denunciation, adopting the hard-left's indispensable tenet while holding their Jewish heads high. Indeed, they can hold their heads even higher than their non-Jewish comrades because they are of such value to the movement.

This could be seen in the Corbyn years, when radical Jewish campaign groups rallied to the old socialist's banner. The high-profile human rights activist Kenneth Roth – whose father was a Jewish refugee from the Nazis – was one of those who rode to his defence. Roth has criticised the Jewish state in particularly lurid terms and campaigned for it to be boycotted. In a controversial letter to the *New York Sun*, he wrote: 'An eye for an eye – or, more accurately in this case, twenty eyes for an eye – may have been the morality of some more primitive moment. But it is not the morality of international humanitarian law.' The paper responded by calling the remark 'a slur on the Jewish religion itself that is breathtaking in its ignorance'. It added: 'To suggest that Judaism is a "primitive" religion incompatible with contemporary morality is . . . the basis of much antisemitism.'[73]

Prior to the establishment of Israel, there was an argument to be made that the Zionist project was ill-conceived. There were factions on both sides. Now that the state is a reality, however, the anti-Zionist position implies the destruction of a living country by undercutting its 'right to exist'. Where should the nine million Israelis go? Into the sea? For a woman to have an abortion is one thing, but to kill a child after it has grown up is quite another. Nobody questions the right to exist of a living person. Nobody, for that matter, questions the right to exist of any country other than Israel, even those like the United States or Australia or South Africa, whose foundation involved true colonialism, ethnic cleansing and genocide.

Related to anti-Zionism is non-Zionism, a position held by many Jews on the soft left. Israelophobia has a way of rubbing off on Jews who crave validation. They start by saying, 'Israel's not my problem', by which they mean 'I don't want Israel to be a problem for me'; and they end up condemning their homeland themselves, like a bullied schoolboy mocking himself before others can do so. If this is the price of acceptance into a world of bigotry, it is depressing how many see it as one worth paying. In a recent interview about antisemitism, the Jewish actor Stephen Fry said: 'I'm not a citizen of Israel. Do I have to tell you how upset I am that the Palestinians are treated so abominably? And how much I dislike West Bank settlements? I don't expect my Gentile fellow Britons to apologise for Putin because he's a Caucasian.'[74]

Fry's remarks conjure up a Jewish state that oppresses Palestinians, thieves their land and is comparable to Putin's Russia. Of course, it is perfectly reasonable to disapprove of 'West Bank settlements', but when your homeland is smeared and attacked unfairly, would it not be right to also speak up in its defence? By insisting instead on his innocence of Israel's heinous misdeeds, all Fry does is concede the heinousness. As a result, he enters a topsy-turvy world: in an interview about antisemitism, rather than standing up against Israelophobia – which after all is the world's foremost expression of antisemitism – he offers himself as its alibi, contributing a Putin comparison for good measure.

That interview was conducted by David Baddiel in 2022. One can hardly accuse the author of the bestselling *Jews Don't Count* of shirking the skirmish. When it comes to Israel, however, he emphasises his lack of connection to the country as a way of bamboozling the haters. 'I don't care about it more than any other country, and to assume I do is racist,' he writes in the book. 'I'm not suggesting that the state of Israel hasn't done many things to be ashamed of. But here's the thing: I am not responsible for those actions and expecting that I should feel so is racist.'[75]

Like Fry, Baddiel makes no attempt to defend the admirable aspects of the country. But in his case, he does so tactically. It means that when he is targeted by those who hate the Jewish state, he is prepared to dodge the blow with a simple response: 'I don't give a fuck about stupid fucking Israel. But I give a fuck about antisemitism.'[76] In his book, he pushes it even further. 'I kind of think: Fuck Israel,'[77] he writes. This has provoked a backlash from parts of the Jewish community, but for Baddiel, it is a way of depriving Israelophobes of a target. 'It so undermines the "you're complaining about antisemitism? It's because you're a shill for Israel" bollocks that so underpins the progressive left conversation,' he told me. 'This has been a principal weapon in me being able to talk about antisemitism in a way that some Jews can't.'

For whatever reason, Israel does not touch Baddiel's heart as deeply as it does for most Jews. Instead, his Jewishness is centred on the diaspora experience. In his book, he writes: 'I am a British person – a Jew, yes, but my Jewish identity is about Groucho Marx, and Larry David, and Sarah Silverman, and Philip Roth, and *Seinfeld*, and Saul Bellow, and pickled herring, and Passovers in Cricklewood in 1973, and my mother being a refugee from the Nazis, and wearing a yarmulke at my Jewish primary school – and none of that has anything to do with a Middle Eastern country three thousand miles away.'[78] Israeli culture leaves him cold. 'Israelis aren't very Jewish anyway, as far as my relationship with Jewishness is concerned,' he continues. 'They're too macho, too ripped and aggressive and confident . . . Jews without angst, without guilt. So not really Jews at all.'[79]

Reading these passages, it feels like Baddiel has substituted Israel – which, as he points out, is 'three thousand miles away' – for an alternative Promised Land that is *four* thousand miles away. His montage of identity may have included some British scenes, but the role models were all American. Perhaps Baddiel, who was born in the United States, was looking for heroes among Jewish comedians and intellectuals, of which there were fewer in Britain. But to me, it seems a short peg on which to hang one's Jewish identity.

While the first Jews arrived in America 350 years ago, Israel was a Jewish homeland since at least a thousand years before Christ. The oldest Hebrew text ever discovered, created in 11 BC, was unearthed at the ancient site of Elah Fortress, near Beit Shemesh, about thirteen miles from

Jerusalem. Can the significance of this be put so easily aside? What about the Western Wall? Or the blue synagogues of Safed? Or the ruins of Herod's palace at Masada, where hundreds of Jews committed suicide rather than capitulate to the Romans? Or the teeming, multifaceted, colourful Jewish civilisation that sprawls vibrantly across modern Israel?

There is no obligation to feel moved by every chapter of your people's history. There may be Italians who feel blank when they see the Colosseum (though I can't imagine those philistines are great in number). But it is a simple truth that Jews have an age-old bond with the Jewish state, whether they are Israeli citizens or not, and whether they feel it or not. Identity is more than a subjective experience. To reject this is to betray more than three millennia of your own culture.

Understanding this, Arab leaders have long waged propaganda warfare on Israel's history. Archaeology has become a deeply politicised matter. In 2000, during the Camp David peace summit, the Palestinian leader Yasser Arafat gave President Clinton a lecture steeped in historical revisionism, claiming that there had never been a Jewish temple on Temple Mount in Jerusalem. 'There is nothing there,' he insisted, wrongly. 'Solomon's Temple was not in Jerusalem, but Nablus.'[80] His successor, Mahmoud Abbas, has amplified the untruth, trying to undermine the Jewish claim to the holy city. As recently as May 2023, he told the UN: 'They dug under al-Aqsa . . . they dug everywhere and they could not find anything.' This misinformation has spread across the Arab world, from the pages of the *al-Jazirah* newspaper in Saudi Arabia to international conferences in the Emirates. It has even been taught at Middle Eastern universities, especially those with an Islamist flavour.

Variations of the lie have sprung up. At the Imam Mohammad Ibn Saud Islamic University in Saudi Arabia, a history lecturer published a paper arguing that King Solomon's temple was really a mosque, despite the fact that Solomon lived 1,500 years before Mohammed was born.[81] It has even seeped into western reporting. In 2003, *Time* magazine said Temple Mount was a site 'where Jews *believe* Solomon and Herod built the First and Second Temples'.[82] As the political scientist and *New York Times* bestselling author Dore Gold recalled: 'In three years, Arafat's campaign had convinced a leading US weekly to relate the existence of Jerusalem's biblical temples as a debatable matter of religious belief rather than historical fact. Arafat had moved the goalposts of historical truth.'[83] Running with the idea, Palestinian officials went on to claim that Jesus was a Palestinian; that Moses was a Muslim; and that the wasteland of Palestine was verdant even before Jewish immigrants famously made the desert bloom. Once again, these narratives have influenced western progressives and international bodies. In 2016, Israel cut ties with UNESCO after it passed a resolution using only Islamic terms for the Jewish holy sites in Jerusalem, airbrushing Jewish history.[84] In short, historical truth is targeted by those who seek to destroy Jewish identity because that is where it is rooted.

There's no reason why Jews shouldn't be 'ripped and aggressive and confident'. The identification of Jews with physical weakness and cerebralism developed relatively recently in the diaspora. With his kvetching and wisecracking and neuroses, Woody Allen bears little resemblance to the swashbuckling Biblical Hebrews in their pre-Christian kingdom. King David, the Goliath slayer, would surely have felt greater kinship with Zionists like Jabotinsky. 'It is long overdue to respond to all current and future accusations, reproaches, suspicions, slanders and denunciations by simply folding our arms and loudly, clearly, coldly and calmly answer, "Go to Hell!"' Jabotinsky wrote in 1911. 'Who are we, to make excuses to them; who are they to interrogate us? What is the purpose of this mock trial over the entire people where the sentence is known in advance?'[85] You can easily imagine King David weighing his sling and nodding. In fact, given Baddiel's heroics against antisemitism, I think he often behaves more like an Israeli than a nebbish American intellectual (in spirit if not in physique).

Perhaps there is something about the Zionist worldview that deadens the sort of comedy he celebrates. As the architects of modern Israel built a new version of Jewish culture, from modern Hebrew to the earthy Israeli character, there was a move to rethink Jewish comedy. Herzl wrote: 'The bad and foolish way we have of ridiculing one another is a survival of slavish habits contracted by us during centuries of oppression. A free man sees nothing to laugh at in himself, and allows no one to laugh at him.'[86] Laughing at oneself is one of the mainstays of diaspora Jewish humour. Could this lie behind Baddiel's stony heart towards Israel? Or could it be that to him, Israelis just feel too culturally distant? Standing up to those who hate your people is always admirable; God knows, Baddiel has enough of a fight on his hands.

In my view, however, the disadvantage of his tactics is that he has vacated the bloodiest battlefield. *Jews Don't Count* dealt antisemitism a stinging blow, but imagine if Baddiel had taken on Israelophobia as well.

Mind your language

Words have power. And when it comes to Israelophobia, using social justice terminology as a Trojan horse for antisemitism makes the old bigotry palatable to the mainstream. People who can no longer malign Jews may speak now of Zionists; they cannot speak of Jewish domination but are free to deride Zionist colonialism; not of Jewish cruelty but of Israeli ethnic cleansing; not of the blood libel of Jews killing Christian children but of Israeli troops being 'happy to kill children', as the BBC put it;[87] not of Jewish superiority but of white supremacy and apartheid; not of Jewish puppetmasters but the Israel lobby. As Jacobson puts it: 'The marauding, child-murdering colonialists of anti-Zionist propaganda are the same hated Jews of 2,000 years ago: separatists, thieves and blood-suckers, long before there was an Israeli soldier patrolling the West Bank. The same calumnies and caricatures proliferate, only this time the Z-word stands in for the J-word.'[88]

As Arendt records,[89] Third Reich documents rarely spoke of deportation, extermination, shooting or killing. Instead, there was 'the final solution' (*Endlösung*). There was 'special treatment' (*Sonderbehandlung*). There was 'evacuation' (*Aussiedlung*). There was 'resettlement' (*Umsiedlung*). There was 'labour in the East' (*Arbeitseinsatz im Osten*). SS troops responsible for the liquidation of Jewish men, women and children were subjected to strict '*Sprachregelung*', or 'language rules' and these euphemisms eased the enlistment of ordinary people in carrying out the most depraved crimes in the name of a supposed greater good.

That's not to draw any parallel between the social justice movement and the Nazis. But the attempt to weaponise terminology has a broad base of adherents, from religious leaders and spin doctors to management consultants, and in the worst hands has been used as a tool of social coercion and murder. As the journalist Andrew Neil has argued: 'Why the obsession with language, with demands for changes in usage which might be thought trivial, irrelevant, even pathetic? Because if you control the language, you've gone a long way to dominating the debate in this new age of identity politics.'[90]

One of the most disturbing phrases of modern times is 'oh, but I'm not allowed to say that'. It implies that a perfectly reasonable and sincerely held position, be it on gender, racial politics or the Middle East, is forbidden in a society that believes itself to be free. You hear this self-censoring attitude with unnerving frequency, around water-coolers and barstools, in cafés, railway stations and sitting rooms. Sometimes you hear its more alarming cousin, '*you're* not allowed to say that', or its mildly subversive relative, '*we're* not allowed to say that'. Those who insist on voicing benign opinions that have become seen as taboo, even though they may be held by the majority, have grown familiar with a common reaction: an agonised cringe, followed by a glance over the shoulder, a pregnant pause, a lowering of the brows and a candid expression of solidarity. In 2021, a YouGov study found that almost six in ten people in Britain silenced their own political or social views because of 'fear of judgment or negative responses from others'.[91] There's a temptation to protest, as John Milton did in 1644: 'Give me the liberty to know, to utter, and to argue freely according to conscience, above all liberties.'[92] Supporters of the Jewish state are certainly familiar with this.

True believers in this new orthodoxy and its linguistic framework, which of course includes Israelophobia, may be relatively few in number, but their influence is powerful. These radical 'progressive activists', as researchers have labelled them – though their activism is more often conducted in boardrooms, on governing bodies and online than on the streets – comprise at least 13 per cent of the population in Britain,[93] but they exert disproportionate power. It is a similar picture across the west. They tend to be wealthy, highly educated and live in capital cities or university towns, where they assume society's most influential positions. Their views are especially radical – or 'hyper-liberal', as the philosopher John Gray puts it[94] – and they are particularly dogmatic and evangelical. They put great effort into cascading their views down through society, via every available channel of influence, from the organisations they lead to the causes they support. Research carried out at Kings College London showed that the progressive activists are six times more likely than anyone else to enforce their political beliefs on social media.[95] In this way, they become self-appointed cultural gatekeepers. Particularly passionate about the rights of minorities, they are overwhelmingly supportive of groups like Black Lives Matter and tend to hold a disparaging view of western history and culture.

The influence of these progressive opinion-formers is profound. Their Gramscian long march through the institutions is setting the tone of our culture and determining what citizens now feel permitted to think. Out of all social groups, they are the most likely to think that the country is structurally racist. Due to the prominent position of Israelophobia among the principles of the movement, experience has shown that when curricula are 'decolonised', speakers are 'cancelled' or pronouns are added to name badges, prejudice against Jews and their national home is never far away.

In 2017, a gay rights Dyke March in Chicago expelled a Jewish woman for flying the rainbow flag emblazoned with the Star of David.[96] The organisers, who ironically promoted the doctrine of 'inclusivity and diversity', said it was because it 'made people feel unsafe'. A subsequent post on the Chicago Dyke March Facebook page complained that it was a case of 'antisemitism masquerading as liberal values'. That was just the start. Intolerance breeds intolerance: at subsequent Dyke marches in San Francisco[97] and Vancouver,[98] feminist lesbians were intimidated and expelled in the name of 'inclusivity'. As the Jewish journalist Hadley Freeman attested after she left the liberal *Guardian* newspaper, the bullying of feminists often goes hand in hand with Israelophobia on the radical left.[99]

The 'apartheid' slur

By making it commonplace, even mandatory, to speak of Israel as an oppressor, the contention that the country is guilty of the worst crimes is adopted without the need for debate. Groups like Amnesty International expend many resources in this effort. Their campaign to appropriate the word 'apartheid' and link it to Israel has involved mass mail-outs, street stunts, official reports and a social media blitz.[100] The logic is straightforward. It is the logic of public relations.

The 'apartheid' charge is one of the main weapons used against Israel and is worth examining more closely. The clearest example of that system, of course, was in South Africa, which enshrined draconian racial discrimination in law. Beginning in 1949, with prohibitions on marriages between blacks and whites, it culminated in laws that reserved the best schools, neighbourhoods, swimming pools, beaches, lavatories and transportation for white people, while black people were corralled into impoverished townships, often in polluted industrial zones, living on subsistence wages and sending their children to overcrowded and underfunded schools. Bullying, arrest, beatings and torture were commonplace.

The period was rife with everything from open savagery to everyday humiliation. In 1960, police gunned down sixty-nine blacks in cold blood during a protest against dehumanising laws that restricted their movement. Black nannies who cared for white children were prevented from sitting with them in church. In his memoir of growing up as a mixed-race boy in a Johannesburg township, the comedian Trevor Noah recalled how 'the only time I could be with my (white) father was indoors', and 'if we left the house, he'd have to walk across the street from us'. Because of his light skin, it was also dangerous for him to be seen with his black mother. 'She would hold my hand or carry me, but if the police showed up she would have to drop me and pretend I wasn't hers,' he wrote. As the black population revolted against apartheid, his township was 'in a constant state of insurrection. Someone was always marching or protesting somewhere and had to be suppressed. Playing in my grandmother's house, I'd hear gunshots, screams, tear gas being fired into crowds.'[101]

Similar examples include the Jim Crow laws in the United States, in which racial segregation legislation was enforced in many states until the 1960s. Black Americans were forced to endure inferior trains, schools, public services and even water coolers. We have seen how Arab countries in the Middle East, which expelled their entire Jewish populations and are dominated by the most appalling racism, often enshrining this in discriminatory laws, are also contenders for the label. The region has several examples of a minority group ruling oppressively over the majority, such as the Alawites in Syria or the Sunnis in Bahrain.

Israel has never been anything like this. It is not perfect – controversy surrounds the 2018 Nation State Law, which enshrined the country's Jewish character – but it is absurd to suggest that its statute books contain apartheid. Far from it. Despite pockets of racism in the country, minorities enjoy legal equality and have risen to some of the highest positions in the land. Six Arabs have been awarded Israel's highest military decoration, the Medal of Distinguished Service, including the legendary Amos Yarkoni, who lost a hand in combat in 1959 but went on to command the elite Shaked battalion. In May 2022, Israel's Supreme Court appointed its first Arab Muslim judge, Khaled Kabub (previous occupants of the court's 'Arab–Israeli seat' had been Christians).[102] Israel's national football team has included more Arabs than Jews in its first eleven;[103] in March 2023, players hoisted Bibras Natcho, their first Circassian Muslim captain, onto their shoulders to celebrate his final game.[104] Arabs have served as diplomats, with Ismail Khaldi, who lived in a traditional tent until the age of eight and grew up tending sheep, becoming Israel's first Bedouin ambassador in 2020. The Israeli Arab Yoseph Haddad fought as an infantryman in the 2006 Lebanon war and almost lost a leg in a Hezbollah missile strike; he recovered and went on to become a speaker and activist, debunking Israelophobic myths on social media.

On the West Bank, it is more complicated. The first important difference is that Arabs in that area are citizens of the Palestinian Authority and live under Palestinian law (including a prohibition on selling of land to a Jew, with a punishment of 'life imprisonment and forced labour').[105] Having said that, it is true that they are subjected to Israeli military apparatus, including checkpoints, and the border with Israel is secured by a barrier. Daily life can be disrupted, for example with the abrupt cancellation of large gatherings due to fears of unrest.

From the Israeli point of view, this is justified not by institutionalised racism but security concerns. The terror threat from the area has long been very serious. Between October 2000 and July 2003, when the first section of the security barrier was under construction, there were thirty-five suicide bombings originating from terrorists from the northern West Bank, killing 156 Israeli civilians. With the first part of the barrier completed, that number reduced to just three in the following year.[106] Once the rest was in place, suicide bombings were practically eliminated.

Check your checkpoints

It is important not to downplay the humiliation of living under intrusive security measures. The worst example is the West Bank city of Hebron, where a main Palestinian road has been permanently closed by the army to protect the Jewish community, and where the extremist Baruch Goldstein massacred twenty-nine Muslim worshippers in 1994. I have seen the chauvinistic Hebrew graffiti on the shuttered shops, and the nets slung overhead in the Arab market, which locals say are to protect residents from rubbish thrown by Israeli radicals. The town, which is home to the graves of Abraham, Isaac and Jacob and their wives, Sarah, Rebecca and Leah, has a history of internecine unrest that long predates the establishment of Israel. In 1929, almost seventy Jews were massacred by Arabs who had been incited to violence by false rumours of Jewish plotting. After that, the Jewish community was evacuated, making the town *Judenrein* until 1967. Today, intense security measures are needed to allow them to live there in relative peace. The 'settlers' are not of my politics, and I stand with the mainstream against any land theft or victimisation of Palestinians. But it must be conceded that opposing any Jewish presence on the West Bank – with its rich and ancient Jewish history – has more than a whiff of apartheid about it.

The original UN partition proposal of 1947 allowed a number of Jews to live in a Palestinian state, just as some Arabs became citizens of Israel. Yet the modern Palestinian government bans Jews from obtaining residency, with harsh penalties for any Arab found guilty of selling land to Jews. Throughout the west, modern liberals support this racist policy. They would not be in favour of laws that ban Hindus from Pakistan, say, or Muslims from Britain, or Mexicans from the United States. How can banning Jews from Palestinian areas be justified, especially given their ancestral links to the area? The situation is much less black-and-white than many people allow. Despite the checkpoints and soldiers, I have seen for myself how in some parts of the West Bank, ordinary Jewish 'settlers' mingle with Palestinian friends and acquaintances at supermarkets. When Rabbi Leo Dee, a British-born resident of the 'settlement' of Efrat, lost his wife and two daughters in a terror attack in April 2023, his late wife's kidney was donated to a Palestinian man, who posed for a picture embracing the bereaved Rabbi. Even in Hebron, in the shadow of terror and zealotry, I have seen soldiers chatting and playing games with Palestinian youngsters.

There are many who argue in favour of reducing such security infrastructure, part of an approach that the Israeli intellectual Micah Goodman has called 'shrinking the conflict'.[107] When lives are at stake, this is a weighty decision. Either way, it is clear that Palestinians are treated differently from Israelis because of their nationality and the security threat, not because of their race. Bullying by Jewish extremists, sometimes with the collusion of soldiers, is a serious problem which is condemned across the Israeli mainstream and must be properly dealt with by the courts. In 2023, there was a spike in revenge rampages by hardline Jews after Palestinian terror attacks, and this filled the mainstream Jewish community with disgust. Yet as ugly and frustrating as the situation is, it does not come close to apartheid South Africa or segregation-era United States.

The best way to expose the falsity of the 'Israeli apartheid' meme is to point out that the allegation preceded the evidence. The slur was in circulation several years before 1967, when not a single settler was present on the West Bank. As early as 1963, the Arab League's London magazine, *Arab Outlook*, included a long essay justifying its economic boycott of the Jewish state by citing 'Israeli apartheid';[108] and in a pamphlet called *Zionist Colonialism in Palestine*, produced by the Palestine Liberation Organisation (PLO) in 1965, a full two years before the 'occupation', the author, Fayez Sayegh, claimed: 'The Zionist settler-state has learned all the lessons which the various discriminatory regimes of white settler-states in Asia and Africa can teach it . . . whereas the Afrikaner apostles of apartheid in South Africa, for example, brazenly proclaim their sin, the Zionist practitioners of apartheid in Palestine beguilingly protest their innocence.'[109] Yet there was no occupation. This was a verdict looking for a crime. Israel's attackers had placed the black cap of the hanging judge on their heads before it was even committed. As we will see in the chapter on Falsification, the slur was invented by Soviet propagandists and hard-wired into both Palestinian thinking and that of leftists in the west, who were accustomed to campaigning against South Africa. In the words of Jean-Paul Sartre: 'If the Jew did not exist, the anti-semite would invent him.'[110]

The South African former judge Richard Goldstone – who was instructed by the UN to investigate potential violations of human rights law in Israel's conflict with Gaza – has rejected the term 'apartheid' outright. In a column for the *New York Times*, he wrote:

> While 'apartheid' can have broader meaning, its use is meant to evoke the situation in pre-1994 South Africa. It is an unfair and inaccurate slander against Israel, calculated to retard rather than advance peace negotiations. I know all too well the cruelty of South Africa's abhorrent apartheid system, under which human beings characterised as black had no rights to vote, hold political office, use 'white' toilets or beaches, marry whites, live in whites-only areas or even be there without a 'pass'. Blacks critically injured in car accidents were left to bleed to death if there was no 'black' ambulance to rush them to a 'black' hospital. 'White' hospitals were prohibited from saving their lives . . . until there is a two-state peace, or at least as long as Israel's citizens remain under threat of attacks from the West Bank and Gaza, Israel will see roadblocks and similar measures as necessary for self-defence, even as Palestinians feel oppressed . . . the deep disputes, claims and counterclaims are only hardened when the offensive analogy of 'apartheid' is invoked.

Even Amnesty International's own senior officials, who are particularly attuned to 'institutional racism', rejected its carefully crafted 'Apartheid Israel' report. Its executive director in Israel, Molly Malekar, objected to the slur, calling it a 'punch in the gut'.[111] She said: 'There is discrimination against Palestinian citizens of Israel, but they have rights, some in key positions; they are campaigning and influencing, and this should be recognised, appreciated and encouraged.' Amnesty's Resource Development Director, Tal Gur-Arye, added on Facebook: 'The claim that this amounts to apartheid does not enjoy a strong foundation in international law, academia, and civil society, let alone the same claim made about Palestinians residing in other countries. My section was not involved in drafting this report, nor in its conclusions and recommendations'.[112]

Apartheid, like the Holocaust, is one of the last things that everybody can condemn, regardless of their politics. That is why it is such a strategically powerful allegation to pin on the Jewish state. It worked to topple South Africa, so it is easy to see why activists expend so much energy trying to attach the same label to Israel. '[Campaigners in the Sixties] successfully sold anti-apartheid as both a human rights issue and a moral cause that everybody could join in with, simply by their choice of which oranges to buy at their local supermarket,' writes British academic Dave Rich. 'It has a mythological status on the left that instantly grants moral authority to anyone who was involved with it. The pro-Palestinian movement has never enjoyed similar support, influence or moral weight, but defining itself as a new anti-apartheid movement could be a route to such status.'[113]

The tactics deployed by activists are clear. Waves of public relations are used to stifle the awkward problem of inconvenient facts, which explains the huge volume of 'apartheid Israel' propaganda online. This is a Trojan horse of anti-racism, in which squats the basest instincts. Viewing this material evokes a grotesque irony. For centuries, Jews genuinely suffered apartheid-style discrimination. These activists are turning the history of anti-Jewish racism against the Jews themselves.

What's your occupation?

The crude word 'occupation' also simplifies a complex and subtle situation. The history alone, which understandably is not widely known, speaks volumes. During the war that followed Israel's birth in 1948, Jordan – which had gained independence from Britain two years earlier – conquered and annexed the West Bank, which had been part of the former Ottoman empire for four hundred years. Jordan retained the territory until the 1967 Six Day War, when Israel defended itself against Arab invasion and ended up winning it. Jewish communities then sprung up, particularly around Biblical sites, and the two thousand square miles came to resemble a patchwork of Israeli and Palestinian settlements amid stretches of wasteland. The planning laws that apply to the area are composed of a mixture of old Ottoman-era legislation and regulations put in place by the British mandate, which existed between 1920 and 1948;

Jewish communities fall under Israeli law. In 1988, Jordan renounced its claim on the West Bank and in 1994, it became the second Arab state, after Egypt, to sign a treaty with Israel, a relationship that was destined to become a 'cold peace'.

That same year, under the Oslo Accords agreements, the territory was parcelled into three areas called A, B and C. While Area C is administered by Israel, the other two are under the control of the Palestinian Authority government – which was set up as a forerunner of statehood – and are home to most Palestinians. Israel is not involved in the administration of the territory, and Israelis are warned not to enter in case they are lynched. In areas A and B, the Palestinians have their own security services and police, their own institutions and their own laws. They engage in their own diplomacy and have a national anthem (*Fida'i*). Arabic language and culture thrive. In short, although Palestine has not yet been recognised as a state pending a peace agreement with Israel, it generally runs its own affairs. There can be no denying that the stateless area is a mess. But it does not always match the impression conjured by the 'occupation' label.

To compare it with a full-fat version, consider Tibet, which has been subjected to a long and brutal Chinese occupation since 1951. The country is now governed directly by the communist government in Beijing, whose forces have full control over the population, administering every aspect of daily life, from tax collection to travel permits. The canton is run according to authoritarian principles, with surveillance, torture and imprisonment without trial accepted as facts of life. Those charged with 'separatism' can face the death penalty. Tibetan language and culture are outlawed and any attempt at expressing Tibetan national identity is crushed. Even wishing the Dalai Lama a happy birthday or having a Tibetan flag on your phone will turn you into a criminal. The anthem and flag are banned and the Tibetan language is being snuffed out in favour of Chinese. The country has been flooded with Chinese immigrants, making Tibetans a minority in their own state. In a particularly chilling move that foreshadowed Putin's abduction of young Ukrainians, up to 900,000 Tibetan children have been separated from their families by the Chinese and are being forcibly educated in colonial boarding schools, subjected to nationalist indoctrination.

Due to Israelophobia, many people assume that the situation on the West Bank resembles that in Tibet, rather than the complicated reality. Whether the term 'occupation' is even appropriate is not a straightforward matter; but although much more can be said on the subject, such a debate lies outside the scope of this book. My aim is to concentrate not on legal technicalities but on popular perception and prejudice. Like the term 'apartheid', using the word 'occupation' has strategic benefits: following the two-step mechanism, it can allow the murder of demonised Jews to be framed as a form of 'resistance'. As we have seen, language has power. When it comes to Israel, nuance is swept away and our very vocabulary is weaponised to destroy it.

The leaders of tomorrow

Progressive ideology is now deeply embedded across the west, in all the institutions run by the elites, from media to academia. It has a powerful influence on the Labour Party in the UK and is heavily represented among the Democrats in Washington. It is a rich irony that despite its focus on anti-racism, the social justice movement harbours a bigotry of its own.

In January, an inquiry into the NUS in the UK[114] found that Jews were being routinely bullied and intimidated on campus. They had been smeared as Zionist agents, excluded for wearing kippot, taunted with 'free Palestine' jeers, stared at and subjected to malicious whispers and comments. Even the fact that NUS identity forms consistently omitted 'Judaism' as an option, when all other faiths were listed, had not been an oversight, the report said. All this harassment was connected to Israel, with activists using pro-Palestine Jews as cover. And there was a clear weaponisation of race-based identity politics.

'[There was a] political agenda being followed by the NUS elected officers who wanted to express their support for the "decolonisation campaign" and to send pro-Palestinian activists towards Jewish organisations campaigning in the same space,' the report said. An official NUS statement blamed the spike in university antisemitism on 'Israeli forces'. Reading the report, it is no exaggeration to conclude that the NUS was in the grip of antisemitic paranoia, cloaked in supposed criticism of Israel.

In one especially illuminating example, black undergraduates had objected to the antisemitism awareness training provided by the Union of Jewish Students. 'Several black women officers have informally let colleagues know that they felt extremely uncomfortable that almost all the examples of antisemitism in the student movement involve women of colour,' the report said. The implication was that antisemitism training was being used by white, Jewish students to intimidate black women and stifle their criticism of Israel. After auditing the sessions, however, the inquiry established that only one example had involved a woman of colour, meaning the allegation was 'without foundation'.

Whether it had been raised maliciously or hallucinated through a form of confirmation bias is not known. But it is revealing that the touchpaper was so easy to light. The report concluded: 'Accepting the complaints of black officers and not investigating or probing them at all seems to show an attitudinal bias of not believing that complaints of antisemitism – if there is any connection at all to Israel / Palestine – are made in good faith.' In other words, when Israel is involved, people go through the looking-glass.

The students of today are the leaders of tomorrow. And they represent just one battalion in the ranks of the social justice movement. Furnished with a degree from a prestigious university and conviction in their worldview, they gain places within society's most important institutions, where they enforce the radical identity politics that leaves most of the country cold. Israelophobia is rolled up into the new orthodoxy that they disseminate through their networks. Because most people do not have the specialist knowledge of

Middle Eastern history and geopolitics required to pick apart the propaganda, a negative view of the Jewish state is easily assimilated. In this way, acceptable antisemitism filters into mainstream society via the schools, universities, left-wing media, museums, galleries, publishing houses, HR departments, advertising agencies, theatres and social media companies that progressives tend to lead. Ordinary people find themselves badgered to subscribe to a narrow set of beliefs on gender, sexuality, race, slavery, colonialism and Palestine, on pain of cancellation. The losers in this equation are always the same: those with unfashionable opinions and the Jews.

Nobody is suggesting that Israel has not sinned. But find me a country that hasn't. During the course of my research, I came across photographs of members of 40 Commando Royal Marines, in full uniform, triumphantly holding up severed human heads during the Malayan Emergency in 1952 (the pictures were suppressed at the time). About twelve thousand were killed in that episode, which was just one of numerous, blood-soaked British campaigns of the period that easily eclipsed the violence of the birth of the Jewish state. Four years earlier, the Arab–Israeli war had claimed between thirteen thousand and twenty thousand lives. Yet whereas Britain's colonial skirmish in south-east Asia is largely forgotten, Israel's founding conflict of 1948 inspires annual commemorations, angry demonstrations and aggressive policy demands to this day. There are many reasons for this, of course. But an important one is hatred, redirected from the Jewish people to their national home.

It is true that Israel struggles with many challenges stemming from religious conservatism and extremism, both Jewish and Muslim. In 2023, several chauvinists found their way into government, causing controversy and consternation; in the coming decades, demographic shifts may place its uneasy coalition of communities under strain, changing the character of the state in ways we cannot predict. But all countries have their problems, just as they have their strengths. It should be unnecessary to point out that for all its faults, Israel is not Nazi Germany, apartheid South Africa, Iran or Putin's Russia. By any reasonable measure, the Jewish state is much closer to the free countries of the west than the autocracies, only with a more turbulent recent history, a different cultural mix and avowed enemies on its doorstep.

Chapter Five

FALSIFICATION
THE THIRD CHARACTERISTIC OF ISRAELOPHOBIA

Parroting the lies of Nazi and Soviet propaganda

The eye of Sauron

Those who are hostile to the Jewish state almost always have no idea that they are parroting propaganda. This is because the lies they peddle – that 'Zionism is racism', that Israelis are 'settler colonialists' and 'white supremacists', that the Jews have become as bad as the Nazis, that Zionists are intent on conquering the Middle East, that Israel is carrying out 'ethnic cleansing' and 'genocide' – were created by state-sponsored disinformation machines, to which massive quantities of resources and commitment were devoted. These campaigns were so successful that even today, people absorb and repeat their messages with no idea of their falsity. This propaganda was produced by the two most oppressive regimes the world has ever known.

It began with Nazi Germany. The falsification of

Israelophobia sprouted in the Arab world in the 1940s, guided by the spirit of the Führer. In the pre-war years, as the dogs of war barked in Europe, harried Jews were fleeing to Palestine. Tensions were running high. Beginning in 1936, the growth of a militant, anti-British Arab nationalism had sparked a bloody Arab revolt, rocking the foundations of colonial rule and forcing London to accept assistance from Transjordan, Iraq, Saudi Arabia and Egypt until the uprising was suppressed. By 1939, there were about half-a-million Jews and twice as many Arabs living under the imperial mandate. The mood was pyretic. In just fifteen months, the triangle of violence between British forces, Arab guerrillas and Jewish militia had chalked up a thousand murders, two thousand sniper attacks, nearly five hundred bombings and more than three hundred abductions.[1] With war approaching, London was concerned about the further contagion of Arab fury.

To prevent it, the Chamberlain government tried to appease the Arab side by issuing a White Paper curtailing its support for Zionism. The terms were threefold: severe restrictions on Jewish immigration, limits on land sales to Jews, and preparations for a single, binational state under Arab majority rule. To the Jewish Palestinians, as they were then known, this was disastrous. By necessity, as the Holocaust would soon demonstrate beyond doubt, the whole point of Zionism was to establish a Jewish homeland with the ability to defend itself; living under the Arabs would simply replicate the experience of the diaspora, which for centuries had been accompanied by convulsions of agony. Then war broke out.

In the Nazi imagination, the Jews were the dark heart of

the Allied enemy. For years, Berlin's propagandists had convinced their domestic audiences that Jewish puppet masters were responsible for the war, accusing them of manipulating Britain, the US and Russia into conflict with the hearty German volk. In 1941, with the Wehrmacht advancing from North Africa towards the Middle East, strategists in Berlin began to consider the value of Islam. If Arabs could be manipulated as the Europeans had been, the Nazis believed they could further inflame the fuel of anti-British nationalism and antisemitism in the region, paving the way for an Allied defeat. In Palestine, despite the fact that Jewish underground militia like the Irgun and the Stern Gang were pitted against British imperial forces, the Nazis felt they could project a similar narrative of the Jews pulling the strings of the British. It was a stretch, but it had worked before. The endgame was clear: if local Arabs turned on British troops and massacred the Jews, Rommel's army, as it marched into the Middle East, would be welcomed as liberators.

To this end, Hitler's propagandists worked to dislodge London's grip on Palestine from the inside. As historian David Motadel revealed, the German diplomat Eberhard von Stohrer called for an 'extensive Islam programme' laying out the 'general attitude of the Third Reich towards Islam'. The essential ingredients were already present. A 1941 memo from Stohrer noted that, 'in Islam, the Führer already holds a pre-eminent position because of his fight against Judaism.'[2] In other words, the existing Arab resentment towards the Jews and their British overlords, combined with an underground reservoir of Muslim anti-Jewish prejudice, was ripe for exploitation. Just as a rich seam of religious antisemitism could be found in the European Christian tradition, an age-old Jew-hatred was embedded in the Quran, an ideal vehicle for the Nazi message. In the years that followed, the hatred that inflamed the Islamic world was a synthesis of indigenous cultural, religious and political roots with the ancient antisemitism of the Christian civilisations, racialised and modernised by the hand of Nazism.

Prior to the Second World War, Jews had lived in Arab lands for millennia. It is true that there had always been undercurrents of anti-Jewish prejudice in Islamic society, where in many cases they were forced to live as *dhimmi*, or second-class citizens. But these had ebbed and flowed, and over the generations, thriving Jewish communities developed across the Islamic world that eventually numbered almost a million. As in Europe, some tried to become almost overly assimilated. In British-occupied Egypt of the late nineteenth century, the nationalist 'Egypt for Egyptians' slogan was coined by the Jewish journalist and cartoonist Yaqub Sanu; the Cairo Jewish community even tried to offer a home in Egypt to Holocaust survivors, to remove the need to emigrate to Palestine.

Although many Jews identified with European colonial powers rather than local nationalist movements, similar histories played out across the region. Libyan Jews made Benghazi into an important commercial hub; Iraqi Jewish intellectuals were among the most important writers of the Middle East; Jewish families in Aleppo used to light an extra Chanukah candle in recognition of the hospitality they felt in Syria; Morocco was once peppered with synagogues, from Tafilalt in the Berber desert to the crannies of the Atlas

Mountains, from Oujda on the Algerian border to Essaouira on the Atlantic coast. Even the mighty Ottoman empire was not known for antisemitism, which at the time was more enthusiastically indulged by Christians.

As the focal point of religious fervour, Palestine had been riven with factional violence for millennia. For four hundred years it had been carved up into various Ottoman *vilayets*, ruled mostly by oppressive Turkish warlords and pashas, rarely by the Arabs or Jews themselves. Despite the frequent bloodshed, there was no intrinsic enmity between Muslims, Jews and Christians in the region. In Jerusalem, despite the almost relentless internecine squabbling, there were times when all three Abrahamic faiths lived side by side in harmony, even participating in each other's religious celebrations. In Europe, meanwhile, centuries of brutal persecution from Poland to Russia, from Lithuania to Romania, popularised a nineteenth-century Jewish movement that sought to establish a homeland in which Jews could live freely and with dignity, develop national pride and defend themselves from aggression.

There had been a Jewish majority in Jerusalem since the 1890s. By the onset of the Second World War, the influx of oppressed Jews dreaming of a country of their own, combined with the presence of British troops, had contributed towards a flammable atmosphere. Bloody clashes had broken out, such as the 1929 massacre of almost seventy Jews in Hebron, and the Arab General Strike of 1936, which led to the general carnage of the Arab Revolt. The violence was volcanic; according to Professor Meir Litvak of Tel Aviv University, more Arabs were killed by other

Arabs in that period than by Jewish and British forces combined.[3] When the Sauron's eye of the Third Reich turned on Palestine and saw this febrility, an opportunity presented itself.

The Lemonade Summit

The power of Nazi falsification stemmed from its ingenuity. Berlin knew that it would not be enough simply to pump its existing material into the Middle East. Even seminal antisemitic texts like the *Protocols of the Elders of Zion*, which had already been translated into Arabic, were felt to be tailored to European culture and sensibilities (though sections of *Mein Kampf* were serialised in Arab newspapers).[4] Hitler's planners knew that if Arabs were to fully assimilate the ideology of the Third Reich, it would need to be presented in a context that felt authentic. In this spirit, a team of prominent Islamists was recruited to collaborate with Nazi propagandists. Leader of the pack was the peacockish Palestinian Grand Mufti of Jerusalem, Hajj Amin al-Husseini, a known extremist who led a gangster war against Palestinian moderates. Recognised as the 'founding father of the Palestinian Arab national movement',[5] Husseini was rather like a proto-Yasser Arafat. For centuries, his family, which claimed to be descended from the Prophet Mohammad, had been one of the most respected local clans, and the Mufti had risen to become the most powerful Arab in British Palestine, controlling a significant budget and network of patronage that included mosques, Islamic courts, schools and endowments (*waqf*).

Since 1936, Husseini – who was by then the leader of his own political movement, the Palestine Arab Party – had been head of the Arab Higher Committee, a ten-member cabal including leaders of all Palestinian factions.[6] He was also a committed antisemite. In September 1937, he had written a 'Proclamation of the Grand Mufti to the Islamic world', which was later recognised as one of the foundational documents of modern Islamic extremism.[7] 'The battle of Jews against Arabs is nothing new,' he wrote. 'The Jews hate Muhammad and Islam . . . Do not rest until your land is free of the Jews.'[8]

The German diplomat Erwin Ettel was Husseini's handler. As Hitler's ambassador to Iran from 1939 until the Anglo-Soviet invasion of Persia in 1941, Ettel had already piloted the harnessing of Muslim antisemitism as a means of curbing British influence in the Middle East. 'One way to promote [anti-British sentiment] would be to clearly connect the struggle of Mohammad against the Jews in old times and that of the Führer in recent times,' Ettel wrote. 'If you combine this with connecting the British and the Jews, it becomes extremely effective.' He and Husseini worked closely together in Berlin, exchanging memos. In one of these, dated 26 June 1942, the Mufti assured his opposite number that Arab and German goals were 'completely overlapping', emphasising that 'the Arabs felt closely bound to the Germans in this struggle against world Jewry'. A victory for the Allies would mean the end of Arab nationalist aspirations, he wrote, whereas an Axis triumph would assure Arab freedom and independence.[9]

On 28 November 1941, the Mufti was granted an audience with Hitler himself. The Palestinian demagogue was taken aback by the honour with which he was received. 'I did not expect that my reception at the famous chancellery would be an official one, but a private meeting with the Führer,' he recalled in his memoirs. 'I had just arrived at the wide square in front of the chancellery and stepped out of the car in front of the entrance of the great building, when I was startled by the sound of a military band and guard of honour composed of around two hundred German soldiers who had gathered in the square.'[10]

The pomp and circumstance of the occasion reflected the esteem in which Hitler held Islam; as Motadel has noted, in his table talks, the German leader would repeatedly compare Christianity unfavourably with the Muslim religion. 'In contrast to Islam, which he portrayed as a strong and practical faith, he described Christianity as a soft, artificial, weak religion of suffering,' he writes. 'Whereas Islam was a religion of the here and now, Hitler told his entourage, Christianity was a religion of the kingdom to come – a kingdom that was, compared to the paradise promised by Islam, deeply unattractive.'[11] Yet the Führer was not in a relaxed mood; the Wehrmacht's advance had just ground to a halt at the hands of the Red army outside Moscow.

Despite the elaborate welcome, the meeting got off on the wrong foot with a disagreement over coffee. In accordance with the Arabic tradition of welcome, the Mufti's interpreter insisted it be served, but Hitler retorted that not even his High Command was permitted to drink it in his presence. Eventually, the Führer left the room and returned with an SS officer bearing lemonade. A well-known photograph and newsreel of the meeting shows the two men deep in conversation, the Mufti serene in robes and turban, the Führer gesticulating on the edge of his seat.

With overweening ambition, Husseini lobbied Hitler to appoint him ruler of an empire comprising Palestine, Syria and Iraq, and grant him his own Arab legion that would fight alongside the Wehrmacht. (He was not the first to entertain such a vainglorious vision. During the First World War, the Hashemite leader Hussein bin Ali, the King of Hejaz in western Saudi Arabia, had offered British forces an Arab revolt against the Ottomans in return for his own empire encompassing Palestine, Arabia, Syria and Iraq.) Hitler put the Mufti's request to one side at first. Instead, he recognised their common enemies – the 'two citadels of Jewish power',

Britain and the Soviet Union – and vowed that there would be no Jewish state. Then he introduced the topic of the Final Solution. 'Germany has resolved, step by step, to ask one European nation after another to solve its Jewish problem,' he said. 'Germany's objective would then solely be the destruction of the Jewish element residing in the Arab sphere.' Finally, he returned to the Mufti's plea for his own Arab empire. It may be considered after the defeat of Russia and Britain, he added, before admiring the Arab's light-coloured eyes and gingerish hair and concluding that he had Aryan blood.[12]

First-class inventors of lies

Though Hitler rejected his request for a further meeting in 1943,[13] Husseini's commitment was assured. In his memoirs, written long afterwards, the Mufti boasted that he had supported the Nazis 'because I was persuaded and still am that if Germany had carried the day, no trace of the Zionists would have remained in Palestine'.[14] He left his meeting with the Führer without any doubt about the Nazi regime's intent towards the Jews. From that day forward, he showed no hesitation about the genocide, later recalling with pleasure that Heinrich Himmler, head of the SS, had told him in 1943 that the Nazis had 'already exterminated more than three million Jews'.[15] A Palestinian delegation visited the notorious Sachsenhausen camp in July 1942;[16] photographs unearthed in 2017 showed Husseini himself on an official visit to a concentration camp in Trebbin.[17] A German official noted: 'The Mufti was a sworn enemy of the Jews and made no secret that he would rather see them all killed'.[18] As Professor Gilbert Achcar put it, '[Husseini] entered into the Nazis' criminal delirium about "the Jews" as it burgeoned into the greatest of all crimes against humanity.'[19]

Himmler developed a close relationship with the Palestinian leader. In a 1943 telegram, he wrote to the Mufti: 'The great Nazi-socialist movement of Great Germany has, from its inception, rebuffed its struggle against world Jewry. For this reason, it closely follows the struggle of the freedom-loving Arabs – especially in Palestine – against the Jewish invaders. The common recognition of the enemy, and the joint struggle against it, are what form the solid foundation between Germany and the freedom-loving Muslims all over the world.'[20] The Mufti agreed; the Arabs were 'natural friends of Germany because both are engaged in the struggle against their three common enemies: the English, the Jews and Bolshevism', he said,[21] offering to assist the Nazis with intelligence sharing and sabotage operations in North Africa. In communications like these, which presented the Jews as 'invaders' and the Arabs as 'freedom-loving', can be seen the first morphing of Nazi antisemitism into Israelophobia.

Soon the project was in full swing. Husseini received a promise from Himmler that after the British were driven out of Palestine, an official from Eichmann's Department of Jewish Affairs would travel with him to Jerusalem to extend the final solution there.[22] Meanwhile, leaflets were distributed in their millions by Axis troops, diplomats, spies and collaborators. Due to high levels of illiteracy across the Arab world, emphasis was placed on the wireless. The task of broadcasting propaganda to the Middle East and North Africa was undertaken by Radio Berlin in Zeesen, a small town south of the capital.

Husseini was placed on the Nazi payroll, receiving nine hundred marks a month. In addition to collaborating on anti-Jewish propaganda, he helped create a German–Arab Legion and a Muslim SS division in Yugoslavia, research by Klaus Gensicke in 1988 revealed.[23] With his talent for rabble-rousing and rejection of attempts to separate religion and politics, the Mufti was an obvious radio presenter and made a number of broadcasts himself; but it was the Head Announcer of Radio Berlin's standard Arabic service, Yunus Bahri, who became an Iraqi Lord Haw-Haw.

Bahri gained great celebrity in the Arab world, despite the limits on short-wave receivers in the war years. 'He is a man famous for nothing more than his dirty tongue, intrigues and a first-class inventor of lies and mischief maker and above all ready to be hired by anyone who pays a good price,' a British intelligence report remarked.[24]

In these diatribes, Middle Eastern aphorisms and passages from the Quran created a homely, authentic feel. The Jewish rejection of Mohammed thirteen hundred years earlier was held up as proof that Jews had always been enemies of Islam; the Jewish desire for self-determination in Palestine supposedly proved that they were equally mendacious in modern times. One 1944 broadcast, uncovered by American historian Jeffrey Herf, a leading expert in this area of scholarship, displayed the typical cocktail of racism and religious fanaticism. 'While the Arabs are lavishly generous, the Jews are meanly miserly,' the announcer intoned. 'While the Arabs are courageous and warlike, the Jews are cowardly and fearful. The differences between the two races were the reason for the enduring enmity which has always existed between them. We therefore believe that this enmity and strife between Arabs and Jews will always be maintained until one of the two races is destroyed.'

The announcer added: 'In Islam, the Jews found a danger to their beliefs . . . They even tried to assault the Prophet.' He then read Sura 5, verse 82, from the Quran, which described the Jews as the most ardent enemies of the Muslims, and claimed they started the First World War to fulfil their dream of a Jewish state 'in Muslim Palestine'.[25]

The basis of this messaging was the age-old demonisation of the Jews. Just as the Germans had been brainwashed for years that Jews were behind all their misfortune, the Arabs were told that they were embroiled in an existential fight against a cunning and repulsive enemy. In 1942, Husseini gave a speech at the opening ceremony of the Islamic Institute in Berlin, in which he both insisted that the Jews had been enemies of Islam since Quranic times and asserted that they controlled both the United States and the heathen Soviet Union.[26]

That same year, an inflammatory vision of Palestine was offered to Middle Eastern listeners. Arabs were living 'in an atmosphere of shame and misery' and 'swimming in a pool of blood', they were told, 'ruled by a reign of terror dominated by the brutal British and the dirty Jews'. Holy places had been violated, they were informed, and plans were being drawn up for the deportation of the Arabs – an invention that belies its origins in the Nazi mind. Britain's war aim was to 'annihilate the Arabs entirely and to aid in this purpose large numbers of Jews are being enlisted in a Palestine army', the broadcaster claimed (in reality, of course, Jews were taking up arms to fight Hitler). For good measure, he added: 'When the Americans seize the British Empire they intend handing over Palestine to their masters, the Jews'.[27]

Interplanetary Jewry

The fact that none of this was true made no difference, as it played to an existing bias. According to British consular reports from Egypt, Arab attitudes towards Nazi Germany fluctuated over the course of the war, but these falsifications left an indelible mark. They can be seen reflected in Israelophobic narratives today, which paint Israel as a colonialist endeavour despite thousands of years of Jewish history in the land, describe Gaza as an Israeli concentration camp rather than a territory ruled by Hamas, wrongly suggest that Israel restricts Muslim access to holy sites in Jerusalem, falsely accuse Israel of perpetrating Nazi-style 'genocide', and talk darkly of the power of the 'Zionist lobby' in manipulating world affairs. In a modern version of the medieval blood libel, Israelis participating in rescue missions in earthquake zones are accused of harvesting the victims' organs. All of this feels true because it is a fresh expression of the oldest hatred, and it was given extra vitality by the Nazis.

With the audience lapping up his falsifications, Husseini and his colleagues made ever more outlandish claims. On 25 April 1941, a Nazi Arabic radio station based in occupied Athens broadcast a programme entitled *Jews in America*.

American Jews, it alleged, owned 98 per cent of the country's banks, 87 per cent of its industry, 97 per cent of its newspapers, 90 per cent of its radio stations, and all its cinemas and theatres.[28]

This was eclipsed only by the hyperbole of a second programme, aired the same day, which suggested that if 'one influential Jew was enough to demoralise a whole country, [the seven million American Jews] could demoralise the whole world and the rest of the planets as well'.[29] As ridiculous as this extra-terrestrial antisemitism may be, it is not a thing of the past. In 2021, Marjorie Taylor Greene, the US conservative who has flirted with QAnon and 9/11 conspiracy theories, suggested that Californian wildfires had profited the Rothschilds and had been ignited by Jewish-controlled 'lasers or blue beams of light' from outer space.[30]

But the propaganda never lost sight of its genocidal goals. In July 1942, as the first Jews were arriving at Sobibor and Auschwitz, a presenter delivered a speech entitled *Kill the Jews before they kill you*. 'Kill the Jews, who have appropriated your wealth and who are plotting against your security,' he ranted.

> Arabs of Syria, Iraq and Palestine, what are you waiting for? The Jews are planning to violate your women, to kill your children and to destroy you. According to the Muslim religion, the defence of your life is a duty which can only be fulfilled by annihilating the Jews. This is your best opportunity to get rid of this dirty race which has usurped your rights and brought misfortune and destruction on your countries. Kill the Jews, burn their property, destroy their shops, annihilate these base

> supporters of British imperialism. Your sole hope of salvation lies in annihilating the Jews before they annihilate you.[31]

In passages like these, you can almost hear the German voice speaking in the Arabic vernacular, stitching together Nazism, Arab nationalism and Islamism to create a Frankenstein's monster of Jew-hatred. It was frighteningly effective. Adulation of Hitler in the Middle East reached a high watermark in 1942, as it reflected the fortunes of war; a Führer heading for defeat was less attractive. However, even those Arabs who disliked him were glued to the propaganda pumped out by Radio Berlin. Meanwhile, London's emphasis remained appeasing the Arabs. Following the principles of the White Paper of 1939, British troops blockaded the dilapidated Jewish refugee ships arriving from ravaged Europe, interning Holocaust survivors in prison camps and deporting them to overseas territories. This continued until the middle of the war, when no more ships came. At the same time, Allied propagandists shied away from mentioning Jews or Zionism in their counter-messaging, for fear of unnecessarily alienating the Arab street.

By 1945, with the end of Third Reich in sight, its ideology was coursing through the bloodstream of the Muslim world. In the Levant, slogans such as *Allah hai, Allah hai, Hajj Muhammad Hitler jai* – Allah lives, Allah lives, Hajj Muhammad Hitler is coming – were chanted. The US intelligence service, the Office of Strategic Services (OSS), a forerunner of the CIA, noted in June 1945: 'Even road gangs in Palestine are alleged to work to the refrain of "*Haj Amin, sayf al-Muslimin*" (Haj Amin, sword of the Muslims) . . .

Nearly every public rally is made to assume the character of a demonstration demanding the Mufti's return.'[32] With the next chapter in the fortunes of Palestine and the Jews about to begin, the ideological ground had already been won by the legacy of the Third Reich.

This same western apathy towards Nazi-Islamist propaganda continued during the Cold War. Indeed, the tendency to turn a blind eye to the presence of such fanaticism in the Middle East continues to this day. Scholarship exposing the legacy of Hitlerism in modern Muslim culture has received little public attention. As the German political scientist and historian Matthias Küntzel argues: 'Knowledge of the connection, embodied in the Mufti, between the Palestinian national movement and National Socialism would complicate the [left's] identification with the Palestinians'.[33] In other words, rather than rethink the Arab role in the conflict, progressives have found it easier to sweep the evidence under the carpet.

After the War, Husseini was captured by Allied forces and held in Paris. But while senior Nazis were tried at Nuremberg, the Palestinian leader was seen as too minor to be included, and Yugoslav attempts to bring him to justice for his role in the SS massacre of the Serbs were unsuccessful. In the Islamic world, 'a pro-Nazi past was a source of pride, not shame', as the eminent historian Bernard Lewis observed,[34] and the Mufti's wartime record did not dent his popularity. There were demands for him to be freed from captivity. Eventually, Husseini was brought to Egypt, where he was given political asylum. In 1954, he published a series of articles in an Egyptian newspaper, which were later compiled as a popular book. 'Our battle with World Jewry . . . is a question of life or death, a battle between two conflicting faiths, each of which can only exist on the ruins of the other,'[35] he wrote. He died in Beirut in 1974.

With friends like these

When 'the Mufti', as he was affectionately known, was granted asylum in Egypt in 1946, one of his allies, Hassan al-Banna, composed a prose poem of praise. 'The Mufti is Palestine and Palestine is the Mufti,' he wrote. 'Oh Amin! What a great, stubborn, terrific, wonderful man you are . . . who challenged an empire and fought Zionism, with the help of Hitler and Germany. Germany and Hitler are gone, but Amin Al-Husseini will continue the struggle.'[36] In 1928, the fanatical Al-Banna – also an admirer of the Führer – had founded the Muslim Brotherhood, the hardline Islamist organisation that would spawn Hamas, and inspire Al-Qaeda and Islamic State. The Mufti belonged to the Brotherhood and actively supported it;[37] indeed, he had been appointed as a leader of the group in absentia.[38] This organisation, which lies at the root of modern jihadism, would become the conduit of Husseini's long and toxic legacy.

In 1949, al-Banna was assassinated by Egypt's secret police. His successor, the firebrand Sayyid Qutb, was even more influential, becoming known as the father of Salafi jihadism. In his twenty-four books and more than five hundred articles, this hugely important extremist intellectual applied his predecessor's ideology to the west, arguing that it was dominated by *jāhiliyyah*, anti-Islamic decadence.

Qutb's extensive writings on Muslim scripture, which were freighted with bigotry towards Jews, the United States, Israel and liberalism in general, were deeply influenced by the Mufti's Nazi propaganda, research by Paul Berman has found.[39] Underpinning the Islamist's worldview was the conviction that the Jews and the societies they supposedly controlled were enemies of Muslims, relying on standard Third Reich conspiracy theories. This propelled Hitler's legacy into the twenty-first century: Qutub's doctrine became the basis of both al-Qaeda and Islamic State.

It was also the basis of the notorious Hamas Charter, composed in 1988. Spanning thirty-six articles, this astonishing document details a comprehensive project of jihad. Research by Küntzel[40] found that it also drew heavily on Nazi propaganda, laying the blame for both world wars at the door of the Zionists and regurgitating old conspiracy theories about Jews, control and wealth. Even without Küntzel's scholarship, so much is obvious. Article twenty-two of the Hamas Charter, for instance, says:

> The enemies have been scheming for a long time . . . and have accumulated huge and influential material wealth. With their money, they took control of the world media . . . With their money they stirred revolutions in various parts of the globe . . . They stood behind the French Revolution, the Communist Revolution and most of the revolutions we hear about . . .
>
> With their money they formed secret organizations, such as the Freemasons, Rotary Clubs and the Lions, which are spreading around the world in order to destroy societies and

> carry out Zionist interests . . . They stood behind the First World War . . . and formed the League of Nations through which they could rule the world. They were behind the Second World War, through which they made huge financial gains . . . There is no war going on anywhere without them having their finger in it.

As if any further proof was needed, article thirty-two – which accused the Zionists of wishing to take over the entire territory between the Nile in Egypt and the Euphrates in Iraq, an area of thousands of square miles – adds: 'Their scheme has been laid out in the *Protocols of the Elders of Zion*.'[41] To describe this as being influenced *by* Nazi propaganda is perhaps insufficient. This *is* Nazi propaganda. The fact that the malevolent ideology of '30s and '40s Germany, so taboo in the west, lies at the heart not just of al-Qaeda and Islamic State but also of Hamas, raises serious questions for those progressives who see the terror group as their friends.

Hitler's ghost

This same ideology has claimed the lives of thousands of westerners. During the 2006 trial of Mounir el-Motassadeq, a surviving member of the 9/11 cell, in Hamburg, a fellow Quran student gave evidence that Motassadeq believed in a 'Jewish world conspiracy' and was convinced that 'the Second World War had been engineered by the Jews so that they could establish Israel'. The World Trade Center killers were particularly interested in New York, the witness added, as they saw it as 'the centre of world Jewry'.[42] Motassadeq's housemates testified that he had boasted about a forthcoming 'big action', gushing: 'The Jews will burn and in the end we will dance on their graves.'[43] As the evidence unfolded, it became obvious that those behind America's worst terrorist atrocity were steeped in the Nazi propaganda that had been delivered to the Middle East by Husseini, and proliferated by the Muslim Brotherhood in the decades that followed.

As Herf concluded: 'The 9/11 attackers were not leftist anti-imperialists. Rather, they were a product, in part, of the continuing aftershock of Nazism in the Middle East. Nazism, which ended as a major political factor in Europe with defeat in 1945, had enjoyed a robust afterlife in the Muslim Brotherhood and its offshoots, such as Hamas and al-Qaeda, which had culminated on 9/11 in an attack on the West, motivated in large part by antisemitic conspiracy theories.'[44]

The influence of the Nazis also explains the genocidal war that was launched against Israel as soon as it was founded. On the face of it, given that the partition of territory between rival ethnic groups was widespread in the twentieth century, the Palestinian rejection of the UN plan stands out. A closer look explains all: the man driving the negotiations on their behalf was none other than the fifty-year-old Mufti Hajj Amin al-Husseini.[45] In the spring of 1947, the UN terminated the British mandate and established a panel to determine the future of the territory. Attempts were made by some UN officials to exclude the Mufti from discussions because of his Nazi past, but these were unsuccessful; as a result, while the Jewish Agency was invited to make submissions on behalf of the Zionists, the bloodthirsty demagogue – who had resumed his pre-war position as the president of the Arab Higher Committee,[46] with his brother Jamal as deputy president – was allowed to represent the Palestinians.

The Arab Higher Committee was dominated by the Husseini clan and their allies, who were in the grip of Islamic extremism. The moderate Palestinians, led by the Nashashibi clan, had been 'left out in the cold' by the Arab League, as historian Benny Morris put it.[47] As a result, the Palestinian side was intransigent from the start, boycotting the UN on the grounds that it was dominated by 'imperialist interests' and refusing to meet envoys in Cairo for talks about partition. The historian Nicholas Bethell recorded: 'Hajj Amin, while he spoke more liberally to British emissaries, made it clear to Arab leaders that, as soon as British forces were withdrawn, the Arabs should with one accord fall upon the Jews and destroy them.'[48]

When the UN offered a Palestinian state alongside a Jewish country – the original two-state solution – the Mufti saw only an opportunity to pursue Hitler's ambition of 'the destruction of the Jewish element residing in the Arab sphere', which the Führer had shared during their private meeting six years before. In an interview with a Jaffa newspaper, Husseini could not have been clearer. The Arabs, he said, 'would continue fighting until the Zionists were annihilated and the whole of Palestine became a purely Arab state'.[49] The wheels were set in motion. Even before the partition plan had been accepted by the Jewish side, Husseini's Egyptian ally, the Muslim Brotherhood leader al-Banna – who since 1940 had been forming special paramilitary units recruited from the Egyptian army – had declared jihad and dispatched a battalion to Palestine.

Behind closed doors, Abdullah I, Emir of Jordan, the Egyptian prime minister Ismail Sidky, the Iraqi prime minister Muzahim al-Pachachi, and even Abd al-Rahman Azzam, the secretary-general of the Arab League, expressed concerns about rejecting the UN plan. But the spirit of pan-Arab nationalism caused regional leaders to take the Palestinian cause as a totem. The Mufti was demanding solidarity and the Arab street, poisoned for years by his propaganda, was in a feverish mood. 'Egypt witnessed the largest pro-Palestinian demonstration in history,' Küntzel recounted. 'Over a hundred thousand people marched through the streets and applauded speakers who expressed their hope that Palestine could be liberated through blood-letting. Jewish and European institutions were attacked and partially destroyed.'[50]

All of this was the direct result of wartime German agitation. Indeed, as hostilities broke out, the Mufti's cries of 'murder the Jews! Murder them all!'[51] could have come straight from one of his wartime broadcasts. The conflict that followed was 'a war of self-defence against a ruthless, pro-Nazi, and openly genocidal Palestinian leadership that enjoyed enormous popularity among the Arab and Palestinian masses', Spoerl observed.[52] Ironically, it wasn't the Zionists who were bent on ethnic cleansing and mass butchery; it was the Arabs. The stage was set. The War of Independence was raging and the Six Day War, the Yom Kippur War, the wider Arab–Israeli conflict and the scourge of jihadism lined up in the future. As Herf writes, 'the rejection of the two-state solution by Hamas, the Islamic Republic of Iran, al-Qaeda, Hezbollah, the PLO, and others remains in part an aftereffect of the fateful fusion of Nazism and Islamism in the 1940s.'[53] Hitler's ghost had a long reach.

To insanity and beyond

The cultural effects of Nazi falsification were devastating in the Middle East. Hitler may have failed to conquer Palestine, but in a few short years he succeeded in formulating the Arab street's widespread hatred of Israel, Jews and the west, which thrives to this day. Even following the German defeat, the Nazi–Arab relationship continued, with former Third Reich officials becoming embedded in Middle Eastern governments. After Israel's tumultuous birth, their Israelophobic conspiracy theories became even more widespread.

In the Islamic world, the lessons learned from the War contrasted sharply with assumptions in the west. From a European point of view, the defeat of Hitler had conclusively discredited antisemitism, with Germany and other countries decisively breaking with the past. The opposite, however, was true of the Middle East. To many Muslims, the establishment of Israel three years after the Allied victory confirmed that Nazi propagandists had been right; the defeat of Hitler had indeed led to a Jewish state in Palestine, helped along by the British. And if they had been correct about that, they could be correct about Jewish ambitions to conquer the rest of the region and annihilate Islam.

Nearly eighty years after the Second World War, a current of affection for Hitler remains among Muslims. Writing in the *Al-Watan* newspaper in 2010, the Saudi columnist Iman

Al-Quwaifli criticised 'the phenomenon of sympathy for Adolf Hitler and for Nazism in the Arab world', which 'turns history in our minds into an imaginary farce in which characters wear masks that contradict the historical truth, and in which good figures wear masks of evil'.[54] Holocaust denial and its variations have also become commonplace. In an expression of startling conceptual gymnastics, it is not uncommon to find Arabic voices saying that had the Nazi extermination programme existed, they would have supported it. A 2002 editorial in the Egyptian state newspaper *Al Akhbar* stated: 'French studies have proven that it is no more than a fabrication. I complain to Hitler, even saying to him from the bottom of my heart, "if only you had done it, brother, if only it had really happened, so that the world could sigh in relief without their evil and sin".'[55] That same year, Egyptian state television and other Arab channels aired a 30-part dramatisation of the *Protocols of the Elders of Zion*, to an audience of tens of millions.[56]

Some Arab media output veers to the point of absurdity. In December 2022, an official newspaper of the Palestinian National Authority *Al-Hayat Al-Jadida* carried the suggestion that Israeli cows were actually 'recruited and trained' spies who wore 'an eavesdropping and recording device'.[57] Similarly, in 2016, Imad Hamato, a professor of Quranic Studies in Gaza, said on Palestinian Authority television: 'The Jews . . . control the media, the money, the press, the resources, the plans.' He later went a step further: 'If a fish in the sea fights with another fish, I am sure the Jews are behind it.'[58]

A major study of a hundred countries by the Anti-Defamation League in 2014 found that 74 per cent of the

Muslims of the Middle East and North Africa, about two hundred million people, agreed with the statements, 'people hate Jews because of the way Jews behave', and 'Jews are responsible for most of the world's wars'.[59] The picture has improved to some degree since then, with a number of Arab–Israeli peace deals, but such embedded trends are not easily reversed. In February 2023, when an Arab-Israeli from East Jerusalem rammed his car into a Jewish family at a bus stop, killing two Orthodox boys aged six and eight alongside a twenty-year-old man, the jubilation was ecstatic. A particularly stomach-churning cartoon in the aftermath of the atrocity showed a Palestinian family – including parents, grandparents and children – gleefully eating the head of one of the victims.[60]

Of course, the Islamic world was not simply a repository for Nazi falsification. The spectacular rise of Israelophobia in the region also flowed from Quranic and cultural antisemitism, resentment of western colonialism, military humiliation in wars with Israel and territorial disputes on the West Bank and in Gaza. As we have seen, pan-Arab nationalism caused leaders across the region to take the Palestinian cause as a totem. But it was the Nazi propagandists and their Arab allies, who strove so ingeniously to match the Israelophobic messaging to the ears of the listener, who established the imagery and turns of phrase that form the lexicon of Israelophobia to this day, and fanned the flames until they became a wildfire.

The Abraham Accords peace agreements in 2020 were a landmark moment in geopolitics. The day after they were signed, the Emirati Islamic scholar Waseem Yousef unleashed a bombastic YouTube broadcast. 'People, let us be frank,' he said. 'It was not Israel that blew up mosques. It was not Israel that incited the Shiites against the Sunnis and bombed the churches of our Copt Arab brothers in Egypt. It was not Israel that gave rise to ISIS. We gave rise to these organisations. We, the Arabs.' In a fiery coda, he concluded:

> Take a look at yourselves before you look at Israel. Take a look at yourselves before you slander peace. Take a look at yourselves, while pointing weapons at one another. You have burned Syria, blown up Iraq, and torn Libya apart. You have divided Lebanon into groups that fight against one another. In Syria, barrel bombs drop on the heads of children . . . You had better just shut up. We are sick and tired of your empty slogans.[61]

But despite the power of interventions like this, in the Middle East, Israelophobia is not the exception but very much the norm.

Over a longer timeframe, there may be some reason for hope. Research carried out for the Tony Blair Foundation in 2022 found more openness in the Arab world than many outsiders assume, with people generally holding similar priorities to westerners, such as secure employment, better educational opportunities and higher quality healthcare. Seventy-five per cent of those polled in Iraq, Lebanon, Saudi Arabia, Tunisia and Egypt believed women should have the same rights as men at all levels of business and government.[62] If traditional attitudes can evolve in some areas, perhaps they can also evolve with respect to Israel.

Across the region, however, from Tehran to Algiers,

hatred of Jews and their national home has long been used by political leaders as a tool of control and strategic advancement. What's more, the 'toxic mixture of Islamism, anti-Jewish hatred, and Palestinian nationalist rejectionism that al-Banna and Husseini implanted' has been projected into the west, where it is consuming left-wing culture and the institutions it dominates. The effects can be seen most vividly in the bastions of the progressives, such as student campuses. '[The Nazi-inspired Muslim Brotherhood] campaigns have had a continuing impact in Western universities, where they serve as the ideological foundation of academic anti-Zionism and the resulting BDS campaigns of recent decades, which have aligned the Western left with the afterlife of Hitler's Nazi Party and its larger designs for the Middle East,'[63] Herf points out. Nonetheless, the Führer's efforts were overshadowed by what came next.

From Russia with hate

Rewind to Israel's fledgling years and the state was the darling of leftists around the world. Even before the Second World War, the *Guardian* editor and progressive politician C. P. Scott was lobbying the British government on Zionism's behalf. 'I was convinced of its value, not only for the Jewish people but for other nations,'[64] he recalled. His position was shared by the Labour Party, which stated in its memorandum of war aims in 1917 that Palestine should become a country 'to which such of the Jewish People as desired to do so may return, and may work out their salvation, free from interference by those of alien race or religion'.[65] Fast-forward to the present, however, and, as the American cultural theorist Susie Linfield put it, 'anti-Zionism has become the almost non-negotiable ticket of entry into left discourse'.[66] What strangled the progressive love affair with Israel? The answer lies in the Kremlin.

Russia, the beating heart of the forces of leftism, had long had a dark and complicated relationship with Jews. The tsarist period had seen an epidemic of antisemitic persecution across the empire, including pogroms, forced conscription of twelve-year-old Jewish boys and the confinement of Jews to the Pale of Settlement (unless they converted to Russian Orthodoxy). As we have seen, the *Protocols of the Elders of Zion* was composed by a Russian agent and promoted by Russian ultra-nationalists. After the 1917 revolution, the Bolsheviks rejected tsarist chauvinism and spoke out against pogroms. Laws were passed banning incitement against minorities and the leadership trumpeted its opposition to antisemitism; but the Soviets opposed religion, and this allowed an opening for the traditional bigotry to creep back in a new guise, as it has done throughout history.

Russia had long had powerful interests in the Middle East, from the Byzantine legacy and the Romanov tsars to the reigns of Catherine the Great and Nicholas I. This continued into Soviet times. Throughout Joseph Stalin's life, he veered among complex combinations of support for the Jews and the basest antisemitism, unleashing mass purges upon them. From 1944, seeing the socialist Zionists as possible allies, he supported their movement. At the time, in Jewish Palestine, leftism was woven into the fabric of life.

Some of the early Israeli political parties and kibbutzim followed openly Soviet policies, and it was not unusual to see people striding about with rifles in their hands and copies of *For Whom the Bell Tolls* in their pockets. After Israel's birth in 1948, Stalin became the first to recognise the country *de jure*. Crucially, he allowed it to procure arms from the Soviet bloc to defend itself from the Arab onslaught that followed.

Following its tumultuous establishment, Israel became a place of dreams, collectivism and idealism, attracting progressive volunteers from all over the world. Stalin's attitude towards the Jews hardened, however, with the seizure of synagogues, forced assimilation and purges of Yiddish-speaking intelligentsia at home. The old hatred emerged more brazenly from the shadows and it became increasingly difficult for Jews to fall on the right side of socialism. Talk of a 'Jewish world conspiracy' became once again commonplace and they were accused of being 'rootless cosmopolitans' who supported 'American imperialism'. Stalin felt increasingly threatened by Soviet Jews' growing enthusiasm for the new state of Israel, fearing it was competing for the hearts and minds of the Jewish proletariat. In 1951, the Russian dictator launched the 'doctors' plot' purges, in which Jewish physicians were sacked, arrested and tortured, and antisemitic and Israelophobic material appeared in the media. The measures only relented – along with suspected plans for the mass deportation of Jews to Siberia – when Stalin died in 1953.

Under the leadership of his successor, Nikita Khrushchev, the USSR switched its allegiance to the Arabs as the Cold War developed, building special relationships with Egypt,

Libya, Syria and Iraq while Israel was drawn into the orbit of the United States. Then came the spectacular Israeli victory of 1967. In one of military history's most audacious episodes, the Jewish state thwarted a second genocidal Arab invasion with a lightning strike that left swathes of territory in Israeli hands, including the Golan Heights, the West Bank and Gaza. Much of it, including the twenty-three thousand square miles of the Sinai Peninsula, was later returned by Israel – itself comprising an area of only about 8,500 square miles – in exchange for peace. But the Six Day War, as it became known, sent shock waves around the region and the world.

The Kremlin received the news with alarm. When hostilities broke out, the USSR had already been indulging in Israelophobia and subsidising the Arab armies; the shock Israeli victory, which meant the destruction of millions of dollars in Russian military hardware, provoked the deepest enmity.

In characteristic fashion, Moscow unleashed the hounds of its formidable 'active measures' against the Jewish state. This was an approach taken by a network of Soviet spy agencies dedicated to manipulating world events through a combination of propaganda and espionage. As retired KGB Major-General Oleg Kalugin recalled, active measures were 'the heart and soul of Soviet intelligence'. In a 1998 interview with CNN, he said: 'Not intelligence collection, but subversion. Active measures to weaken the West, to drive wedges in the Western community alliances of all sorts, particularly NATO, to sow discord among allies, to weaken the United States in the eyes of the people of Europe, Asia,

Africa, Latin America, and thus to prepare ground in case the war really occurs.'[67] A well-known example was Operation Infektion, which sought to convince the world that HIV had been invented as a biological weapon by the Americans. In 1987, this fake news was famously reported by CBS.

The first Israelophobic salvo came from the Kremlin in August 1967, less than two months after the end of the war. An identical article appeared simultaneously in numerous publications, under the headline 'What is Zionism?'. Written by Yuri Ivanov, one of the fathers of the new campaign, it falsified Israel as the expression of a fabulously funded, international Jewish plot that controlled politics, media and financial markets across the world. The shared Nazi roots were obvious, as was the influence of the *Protocols of the Elders of Zion* and older antisemitic tropes. The snowball of Israelophobia was set rolling, and it was only a matter of time before university campuses, gender and environmental activists, trade unions and the entire edifice of global leftism would be caught up in the avalanche.

Meet the Zionologists

Between 1967 and about 1988, the KGB embarked on a massive disinformation campaign called SIG, short for *Sionistskiya Gosudarstva*, or 'Zionist Governments', which flooded the world with Israelophobic paranoia, this time moulded around the Soviet worldview and objectives. The KGB chief driving the project was Yuri Andropov, who later briefly became leader of the country until his death in 1984. Beneath the surface, this softly spoken, urbane intellectual harboured a stony ruthlessness, coupled with hardline views and an enthusiasm for crushing dissent. It is no exaggeration to call him the father of modern Israelophobia. Ironically, after his death it emerged that he had hidden his Jewish heritage all his life.

SIG was a mind-bogglingly sophisticated operation. Lieutenant-General Ion Mihai Pacepa, former head of Romanian intelligence and the highest-ranking spy ever to have defected from the former Soviet bloc, was one of those responsible. '[Our] task was to export a rabid, demented hatred for American Zionism by manipulating the ancestral abhorrence for Jews felt by people in [the Middle East],'[68] he recalled. Despite all this bigotry, the Soviets – just like the Israelophobes of today – claimed that they had no objection to Jews who conformed to their ideals, meaning that they were not antisemitic but only 'anti-Zionist'. (In 1979, the *Washington Post* called this 'a distinction without a difference'.)[69]

The group of right-wing ideologues who produced ideas for the new falsification campaign were known by the strange name 'Zionologists'. Even though they lived in the USSR and worked for the communist regime, many held older, xenophobic and Russian ultranationalist views, which they learned to express in Marxist–Leninist terms. Antisemitism was still officially prohibited in the country, so the messaging was moulded to Soviet standards. Borrowing heavily from *The Protocols of the Elders of Zion* and Hitler's *Mein Kampf*, they set about pinning their messages to the new gospel. As the Zionologist Vladimir Bolshakov recalled in his memoirs, his influential colleague Ivanov 'managed to supply a strong theoretical foundation for openly criticising Zionism with the help of Marx's and Lenin's works, which no one could argue against.'[70]

The seamless contiguity between far-right and left-wing agitprop was neatly exposed in 1973, when a Paris court convicted Robert Legagneux, a member of the French Communist Party and employee of the Russian embassy in Paris, for inciting racial hatred. His crime had been to publish anti-Zionist propaganda in a leftist French magazine controlled by the embassy. It contained typical disinformation: Israel was equated with Nazi Germany and accused of throwing Arabs 'into ghettos, behind the barbed wire of concentration camps'; Judaism was alleged to have preached the racial superiority of the 'God-chosen people',[71] brainwashing Israeli children to kill non-believers. During the trial, it sensationally emerged that the supposedly leftist article included entire passages, complete with typographical errors, lifted from a far-right 1906 pamphlet by a member of the Black Hundreds sect, which had been responsible for inciting pogroms in tsarist Russia. The word 'Jew' had simply been replaced with 'Zionist'.

The propaganda effort involved millions of newspaper articles, radio broadcasts and books. The founding text of Soviet Israelophobia, *Beware: Zionism!* by Yuri Ivanov, was released in 1969 and reprinted multiple times. Selling 800,000 copies, it was produced in at least sixteen languages, from English, Arabic and French to Polish, Ukrainian, Estonian and Slovak. It falsified Judaism as a vicious and inhuman religion that had spawned fascist Zionism. 'In Israel, and especially in the occupied territories, the Zionists have unleashed open terror against the Arab population,' it claimed. 'This terror takes various forms, but all of them are reminiscent of the methods employed by the Nazis during the Second World War.' Jewish dreams of self-determination in their ancient homeland were portrayed as a global threat. 'Wherever it possibly can, international Zionism (by no means always acting under the Israeli flag) tries to undermine the prestige of the socialist countries and organise both petty acts of provocation and major ideological subversion against them,' the book ranted. It concluded with a throwback to old-school antisemitism: 'Everywhere there are people who do not doff their caps before the owners of bulging purses and extensive kennels and will not permit them to lurk in the shadows again, just as nations and history will not permit them to escape retribution.'[72] This set the tone for a tsunami of Soviet disinformation that would sweep the world.

Ivanov was the ringleader of about a dozen prolific Zionologists who together unleashed a wave of books that sold millions of copies. A typical title was Yevgeny Yevseyev's *Fascism Under the Blue Star*; in a sign of the way the Soviets adapted their messaging to the mores of their audiences, its English edition was cleverly reprinted in the '80s as the trendier *Racism Under the Blue Star*. Even children were targeted. In 1983, the Soviet publishers Pedagogika released a book aimed at teenagers[73] called *The Poison of Zionism*, which was filled with antisemitic illustrations. Written by Yelena Modrzhinskaya, a former intelligence officer, the first print-run alone produced 200,000 copies. Every Israelophobic Soviet publication was amplified with numerous reviews and articles aimed at specific audiences such as soldiers, party apparatchiks, trade unions and youth groups.

Almost all the disinformation contained in this material is alive and well in the twenty-first century. The heavily *Mein Kampf*-inspired *Zionism and Apartheid*, for example, put forward the apartheid smear that is now depressingly commonplace. In February 2023, just after Holocaust Memorial Day, the left-wing Labour MP Kim Johnson was forced to apologise after asking in the Commons: 'Since the election of the fascist Israeli government last December, there has been an increase in human rights violations against Palestinians, including children. Can the Prime Minister tell us how he is challenging what Amnesty and other human rights organisations refer to as an apartheid state?'[74] It later emerged that a Labour parliamentary candidate, Faiza Shaheen, had said in an interview: 'If you can't say that Israel is an apartheid state, or if Palestinians in this country can't say that it was racist, without being labelled antisemitic by the Labour Party, then I think there is a problem.'[75]

It is striking to see this Soviet-era piece of disinformation persisting in the British parliament, despite the absence of fascism and the two million Arabs living freely in Israel – one of whom, Samer Haj-Yehia, happens to be chairman of the country's biggest bank – and the four hundred mosques in the country. (By contrast, there are zero Jews, bankers or otherwise, and zero synagogues in the Palestinian-controlled territories.) It is likely that Amnesty International, which has officially endorsed this Soviet Israelophobic agitprop, and supporters like Johnson and Shaheen, have no idea that they are parroting old Kremlin falsifications.

Moscow's efforts were even more wildly successful than

those of Berlin two decades before. Izabella Tabarovsky, the world's foremost expert on the subject, whose research has revealed the true extent of Soviet Israelophobia, stressed how the campaign 'succeeded at emptying Zionism of its meaning as a national liberation movement of the Jewish people and associating it instead with racism, fascism, Nazism, genocide, imperialism, colonialism, militarism and apartheid'.[76] In short, every single one of the myriad levers available to the Kremlin was pulled in the service of Israelophobia. Combined with the ancient antisemitic assumptions that already underpinned global attitudes towards Jews, this set off butterfly effects across the globe that continue to warp the debate today, even in the mother of parliaments.

Guns and olive branches

The evolution from medieval antisemitism to Nazi racism, Soviet disinformation and modern Israelophobia is all too obvious. Each new ideology comfortably co-opts the tropes, images and principles that came before, pushed by powerful states. Whereas the Nazis wove a web of evil around Jews, the Soviets talked instead of the Zionists. Into the *dezinformatsiya* machine went the medieval bigotry against the Christ killers, mixed with Nazi ideas of the 'dirty Jew'; out of it came the Zionist as an enemy of the left. In went the Jew as a devil; out came the Zionist as a Nazi.

Conspiracy theories remained at the heart of the bigotry. Ultranationalist and Third Reich rhetoric was grafted onto Marxist–Leninist discourse, with the portrayal of Jews as international bankers controlling finance, politics and the media requiring only the thinnest of Soviet veneers. Zionists were accused of stoking antisemitism and even orchestrating the Holocaust to strengthen their case for a Jewish state – then told they were using that same persecution to stifle criticism. Judaism was portrayed as a malevolent cult that inspired acts of cruelty. In the last two decades of the Soviet empire, the KGB's calculated untruths infected progressives all over the world, becoming a permanent part of left-wing thinking. From there, it spawned into institutions, from fraternities of American colleges to the corridors of the British Parliament to continental newsrooms. The influence of the radical elites has helped cascade it into the contemporary mainstream, meaning that in the second decade of the twenty-first century, Israelophobia is thriving.

Like the Nazis before them, a major target of the Russian campaign was the Middle East. In the '70s, the KGB showered Muslim countries – already softened up by the Mufti and his Nazi handlers – with an Arabic translation of the *Protocols of the Elders of Zion*. Russian spies made documentaries in Arabic supposedly proving that Israel and the United States were Zionist entities dedicated to creating a Jewish colony across all Muslim lands,[77] another obvious echo of Nazi ideas. Spies infiltrated the region with the sole objective of spreading Israelophobic agitprop. As Lieutenant-General Pacepa recalled, '[My agency] dispatched around five hundred such undercover agents to Islamic countries. According to a rough estimate received from Moscow, by 1978 the whole Soviet-bloc intelligence community had sent some four thousand such agents of influence into the Islamic world.' When the USSR supported Muslim countries by constructing hospitals, housing and infrastructure, it instructed its engineers, technicians and doctors to spread one message: the United States was an arrogant Zionist imperialist and colonialist power, financed by Jewish money and run by Jewish politicians, which aimed to subordinate all Muslim lands.[78]

Vast numbers of cartoons were churned out using classic Nazi imagery of Jews as spiders, dogs, octopuses, snakes and bloodsuckers. In a final insult, they were also depicted as Nazis. These illustrations were sent out worldwide, in many languages, and still appear in western media from time to time; but in another demonstration of the influence of the Middle Eastern propaganda campaign, they remain widespread in Arabic cartoons today.

The Arab world, which by now harboured a deep, Nazi-inspired hatred of the Jews, readily cross-fertilised with the Soviet mutation. Ever since its founding in 1964, the Palestine Liberation Organisation (PLO) claimed the leftist revolutionary narrative, casting Israel as an outpost of western imperialism rather than an expression of Jewish self-determination. The Palestinian leader Mahmoud Abbas studied for his PhD at Patrice Lumumba University in Moscow, now People's Friendship University of Russia. The director, Yevgeny Primakov, was a mastermind of 'active measures' who was involved in the HIV disinformation campaign Operation Infektion.

In Abbas' 1982 dissertation, *The Connection between the Nazis and the Leaders of the Zionist Movement*, the KGB influence is clear. It is a bizarre piece of historical falsification, claiming that Zionists engineered the Holocaust as a pretext to establish Israel in Palestine. In one notorious passage, he wrote: 'The Zionist movement led a broad campaign of incitement against the Jews living under Nazi rule, in order to arouse the government's hatred of them, to fuel vengeance against them, and to expand the mass extermination.'[79] He went on to argue that no more than one million Jews had been killed in the Holocaust, but the Zionists had inflated the numbers to win more sympathy for their cause. In a particularly outlandish move, he alleged that Israel had only seized and tried Adolph Eichmann, the architect of the Final Solution, to prevent him revealing the Zionists' role in the genocide. As if by coincidence, a year later the very same claims were made publicly by Soviet apparatchiks.

Similarly, Yasser Arafat, who enjoyed a close relationship with the USSR, repeated Israelophobic disinformation almost word-for-word in speeches at the UN. In his famous 1974 'gun and olive branch' address to the General Assembly, for example, he railed against 'imperialism, colonialism, neo-colonialism and racism, the chief form of which is Zionism'. The nadir came in 1975, when after nearly a decade of Arab and Soviet lobbying, the UN passed General Assembly Resolution 3379, ventriloquising the central agitprop motif that 'Zionism is racism'. For years, the Kremlin had been trying to persuade the world that Zionism was an expression of Jewish racial superiority, a modern manifestation of a supposed 'chosen people' complex. The UN resolution was a propaganda achievement even more impressive than AIDS disinformation appearing on CBS. As the *Spectator* journalist Goronwy Rees despairingly reflected: 'The fundamental thesis . . . was that to be a Jew, and to be proud of it, and to be determined to preserve the right to be a Jew, is to be an enemy of the human race.'[80] The resolution, which prompted British Students' Unions to ban Jewish societies on campuses, was only repealed in 1991.

By 1973, when shipments of US weapons helped Israel to narrowly survive the Yom Kippur War, the arena had become a full-on proxy conflict for the warring superpowers. With Soviet propaganda buzzing in their ears, western leftists whose sympathies lay with the Reds turned their backs on the Israeli dream. The Zionist project had gone from the repatriation of an indigenous people to a conquest by western capitalists. Arabs were recast as revolutionaries fighting imperial masters. With the collapse of the British Empire, a loathing of colonialism became a marker of progressive political identity, and this paradigm was imposed on the Israeli–Arab conflict, regardless of how badly it fitted. The word 'Palestinian', which had previously applied to both Arabs and Jews of the country, now described only the Arabs, making it easier to project a narrative of white supremacists oppressing native people.

Moscow goes global

Whereas Nazi Israelophobia had been limited to the Arab sphere, the Kremlin also projected its version worldwide. This is the main reason why it remains so influential in the west today. Tabarovsky has revealed the vast extent of the propaganda campaign, which remains little-known by the mainstream, especially among those who continue to parrot it. The operation was coordinated by Novosti Press Agency, the Soviet state organisation later reincarnated as *Russia Today* or *RT*. Staffed by journalists and propagandists, many of whom had ties to the KGB, it was active in 110 countries.

In addition to the growing library of Israelophobic books, tens of millions of copies of newspapers and magazines were printed each year in eighty languages, including English, French, Spanish, German, Arabic and even Hindi. Pocket-sized pamphlets were distributed all over the world with titles like *Deceived by Zionism*, *Zionism Counts on Terror* and *Criminal Alliance of Zionism and Nazism*. Radio Moscow's foreign broadcasts put out thousands of hours of programming every month, including in Hebrew. Taking their cue from the Nazis, they adapted their messaging to different cultures. On one day in 1973, African listeners were bombarded with messages in French, English and Portuguese claiming that Zionism had 'an ideological affinity with South African racism', a falsification that is commonly spouted by Israelophobic activists today. In Latin America, Zionism was linked with American imperialism; in Asia it was elided with fears of postwar Japan.

In true 'active measures' style, radical leftist groups in the west were used to further Russian interests, galvanise supporters and infect overseas audiences with Israelophobia. Sometimes, these networks would manage to get Soviet propaganda played on local radio stations or printed in the papers. Moscow pumped huge sums of money into these front organisations across the globe. Between 1950 and 1990, the French Communist Party received US$50 million, plus free printing for its newspaper *L'Humanité*, as well as expenses for its Moscow correspondent. The British Communist Party's *Morning Star* paper, for which Jeremy Corbyn was a columnist, also benefited from Soviet funding. (The man who became his political adviser when he was Labour leader, Andrew Murray, both wrote for *Morning Star* and worked directly for Novosti.) These relationships had been decades in the making. In 1940, Orwell wrote that the English intelligentsia 'take their cookery from Paris and their opinions from Moscow'.[81] During the Cold War, these imported Soviet opinions became poisoned with Israelophobia.

The tempo of the output was intense. In 1970, *Soviet Weekly*, a Russian propaganda newspaper targeting Britain, serialised a potent Israelophobic story across four consecutive issues. It described Zionism as 'not so much the Jewish nationalist movement it used to be but an organic part of the international – primarily American – imperialist machinery for the carrying out of neocolonialist policies and ideological subversion'.[82] Later, the same magazine ran an article entitled 'Why We Condemn Zionism', which branded Jewish nationhood a racist doctrine and claimed that Israelis were 'worthy heirs to Hitler's National-Socialism'.[83] As we have seen, the vitriol in these publications was sometimes indistinguishable from that of the antisemitic far-right. In 1980, the newspaper of the British Socialist Workers Party was left red-faced after it published a letter from a leader of the fascist National Front, having mistaken his Israelophobic tirade for that of a leftist.

Other Russian propaganda publications in Britain included the 1979 newspaper *Straight Left*, whose star columnist, Andrew Rothstein, was an active Soviet agent (the paper was managed by Seumas Milne, who later rose to prominence as Corbyn's spin doctor). It was saturated with Israelophobia. Palestinian terror against civilians was repeatedly praised, framed as a revolutionary struggle. 'The PLO has found great support in the Third World and the socialist camp, with the USSR at its forefront,' it gushed. The Iranian revolution, which was a victory for the fascist theocracy, was applauded, described as an 'anti-imperialist people's struggle for independence, freedom and social justice'. When the Iranians took fifty-two Americans hostage in Tehran in 1979, *Straight Left*'s hot take was that it was 'an excuse for the creation of another wave of anti-Iranian hatred'.[84]

A direct line can be drawn from Kremlin agitprop through

publications like *Soviet Weekly* and *Straight Left* to the social media rants of the contemporary hard-left. This was particularly evident when Jeremy Corbyn was leader of the Labour Party. At the time, on a Facebook page entitled 'Jeremy Corbyn Leads Us to Victory', a former Labour candidate posted an Israeli flag defaced with a swastika, a classic of Russian propaganda. On another, a Labour figure posted a picture of *New York Times* journalists with their faces covered by Jewish symbols, implying that they served a Zionist agenda. Another called Hitler 'the greatest man in history', adding 'it's disgusting how much power the Jews have'; another commented, 'it's the super-rich families of the Zionist lobby that control the world'; another called the six million Jewish victims of the Nazis 'a big lie', repeating the Holocaust denial that was another key feature of the Russian disinformation campaign.[85] The Cold War propagandists had been frighteningly effective.

In the United States, Soviet Israelophobia flowed along conduits like the Communist Party USA, which received US$28 million from Moscow between 1958 and 1980. A particular win came in 1971, Kremlin memos reveal. A Novosti article exploring 'the spiritual kinship of Zionism and fascism' – arguing that every American Jew linked to Israel was a 'Zionist fanatic' and fifth columnist obstructing American–Russian peace – made it into the *New York Times*, America's paper of record. Headlined *A Soviet View on Jews*, it was presented as part of a debate expressing both sides. But the goal of the article was achieved: to introduce the 'Zionism is Nazism' smear to the *Times*' large and influential readership.[86]

Memos also reveal that in the early '70s, Hyman Lumer,

editor-in-chief of *Political Affairs*, the American Communist Party journal, travelled to Moscow to receive 'materials for unmasking the Zionist anti-Soviet campaign' for 'wide distribution within the US'.[87] His subsequent work, including a 1973 book entitled *Zionism: Its Role in World Politics*, shrewdly sidestepped antisemitic tropes that would offend Americans while focusing on the bigotry of Israelophobia. To this day, the US's Communist Party continues in the same vein. At its 2010 convention, delegates debated the motion: 'Zionism is a form of racism, and racism has no place in our Communist Party!' A preliminary article unequivocally stated that 'Zionism is racism and genocide'. It went on: 'Zionism is not only a virulent strain of bourgeois nationalism, of kinship with South African Apartheid. Not only is it an anti-working-class diversion in the Middle East. Zionism is a roadblock to building working class unity in our country.' US communists must work to 'consign Zionism to the rubble of history', the article concluded.[88]

Given the gargantuan efforts put into funnelling such volumes of propaganda to worldwide audiences, it is perhaps no surprise that Israelophobia maintains such a grip on the international left today, as well as the institutions it dominates.

They don't even know it

Part of the reason for the huge resources poured into active measures against Israel was that it helped the USSR to achieve its foreign policy objectives. As Tabarovsky writes: 'Antizionism helped Moscow bond both with its Arab allies and the Western hard left of all shades. Having appointed

Zionism as a scapegoat for humanity's greatest evils, Soviet propaganda could score points by equating it with racism in African radio broadcasts and with Ukrainian nationalism on Kyiv TV.' As a sign of the diplomatic objectives of Israelophobic disinformation, teams of Zionologists were supervised by Ivan Milovanov, head of the Kremlin's Middle East section, who personally rubber-stamped all output on 'international Zionism'.[89]

Diplomatic leaders from the developing world who visited Moscow were assured of goodwill if they joined in condemnations of 'imperialism and Zionism', while Russian embassies overseas covertly disseminated the toxic disinformation. In the early '70s, the Soviet ambassador to Washington, Anatoly Dobrynin, set up a special propaganda council at the embassy in DC. Its aims included: shearing off public support for the Jewish state; causing people to question the loyalties of 'Zionists'; driving a wedge between the governments of the United States and Israel; and convincing the US public to abhor 'the brazen face of the leaders of the newly-minted Zionist "higher race" from Tel Aviv'. Parallel KGB operations worked to sow division between Jews and blacks in America and undermine Jewish communities.

These efforts were bolstered by worldwide Soviet sympathisers. Whether he did so cynically, in earnest or simply by osmosis, the revolutionary icon Che Guevara – who visited Gaza in 1959 – made his own contribution to the spread of Israelophobia. In 1967, in an article for Britain's *New Left Review*, he mapped out the struggle between 'imperialism' and socialists across the globe. When he came to the Middle East, he offhandedly described 'Israel, backed by the imperialists, and the progressive countries of that zone'. This was 'just another of the volcanoes threatening eruption in the world today',[90] he wrote. In reality, of course, the Jews were not a tool of imperial powers but a wandering people with indigenous roots seeking to form a postcolonial state. And the Arab countries were among the least 'progressive' in the world. But when ideology comes first, reality makes little difference.

In 1990, just before the USSR collapsed, its official newspaper, *Pravda*, published a belated *mea culpa* of sorts. 'Considerable damage was done by a group of authors who, while pretending to fight Zionism, began to resurrect many notions of the antisemitic propaganda of the Black Hundreds and of fascist origin,' it admitted. 'Hiding under Marxist phraseology, [propagandists] came out with coarse attacks on Jewish culture, on Judaism and on Jews in general.'[91] But it was too late. The virus had been released and had taken on a life of its own. As Dr Jovan Byford, the psychologist and conspiracy theory expert, pointed out, it had reached the point where 'the far-left in Britain and on the Continent viewed Middle Eastern politics almost exclusively through the prism of Soviet anti-Zionism.'[92]

Today, the similarity between the worldview of modern leftists and Soviet falsification of the period is breathtaking. It is no exaggeration to say that almost all of the Israelophobic tropes in current circulation – that Israel is a racist state, that Zionism is colonialism, that genocidal Israelis are no better than the Nazis, that Israel practises apartheid, that the Holocaust was exaggerated, that diaspora Jews are a fifth column serving Israeli interests and so on – were disseminated by Soviet spin doctors, based on works of classic antisemitism like the *Protocols of the Elders of Zion* and Hitler's *Mein Kampf*.

Largely because of Russian efforts, many otherwise well-meaning progressives don't see what's wrong with accusing Israel of subjecting the Palestinians to a Holocaust, despite, say, the lack of gas chambers, execution pits or Nazi-style racial discrimination laws in the Jewish state, not to mention the growing Palestinian population. They don't see what's wrong with using the slur 'apartheid', even though in recent years, an Arab Muslim judge imprisoned a Jewish former prime minister for corruption. (If you visit the West Bank, you will come across large, red signs outside Arab areas warning Israelis not to enter for their own safety. It is hard to sustain the argument that Israel – rather than its neighbours – is the apartheid state.)

They happily compare Zionism to imperialist colonialism, ignoring the fact that the Jewish pioneers were not an invading army but a ragtag collection of refugees, dreaming of self-rule in their ancestral home after millennia of life at the mercy of the mob. (As Herzl put it, they simply wanted a place 'where it is all right for us to have hooked noses, black or red beards, and bandy legs without being despised for these things alone. Where at last we can live as free people on our own.'[93] Hardly the sentiments of white supremacist imperialists.) They take for granted that 'Zionism is racism', unaware that this phrase was cooked up in Cold War Moscow and does not survive contact with reality. Even the fact that 'Zionist' has become a dirty word in certain quarters today points to the skill of the Soviet propaganda apparatus and the KGB.

In the minds of millions around the world, Soviet agitprop succeeded in redefining Zionism from an answer to millennia of persecution to a bourgeois, imperialist project. In this way, it wiped antisemitism clean, allowing progressives to indulge an old hatred by convincing themselves that they were merely taking a principled stand against Israel. Across the decades, the Cold War communists and contemporary Israelophobes both say: we're not antisemitic, just anti-Zionist. But theirs is a deep and ancient bigotry, resting on disinformation and paranoia. Nearly six decades on, Soviet Israelophobia continues to grip the modern left. It finds an easy target in those lacking knowledge about Israel, Zionism and Jews, and possessing impulses inherited unchallenged from previous centuries.

Here comes Tehran

It is easy to wonder why the Iranian regime is so obsessed with the Jewish state. Not only do the two nations have no border or bilateral dispute but they are some thousand miles apart. They have enjoyed close relations in the recent past and Jews have lived in Persia for 2,700 years; large segments of the Iranian population remain well-disposed towards Israel. However, after seizing power in the revolution of 1979, Ayatollah Ruhollah Khomeini positioned his regime as the champion of the emotive Palestinian cause, tempting Sunni states to rally behind his Shia leadership, extending Tehran's influence and undermining unfriendly states. Moreover, the prophecy of the coming of the Mahdi messiah, central in his brand of Islam, involved an apocalyptic battle with the Jews; and focusing his population's attentions on the Jewish Satan presented a useful distraction from the poor living standards, corruption and repression they were enduring. For these reasons and others, he seized the opportunity to become the world's foremost standard-bearer for Israelophobia.

Today, the Iranian regime pumps out huge volumes of sophisticated, multilingual Israelophobic propaganda, which is seeded and cultivated worldwide, largely via the internet. Hundreds of Tehran-based websites and many thousands of social media accounts spew out this disinformation, sowing Israelophobia and discord in the west. The sites and accounts which, in the course of my journalism, I forensically traced to the Islamic Revolutionary Guard Corps, routinely disseminate material such as cartoons of bloodthirsty Israeli soldiers in league with Saudi Arabia and the United States, and extensive Holocaust denial – targeted as the Holocaust is often taken to demonstrate the reason for Israel's existence.[94]

In a pattern that will by now be all too familiar, Iranian Israelophobia is accompanied by attempts to destabilise British society. Proxy accounts praised leftist firebrands George Galloway and Rebecca Long-Bailey, attempted to undermine the BBC over its coverage of Prince Philip's death, and carried cartoons showing British missiles fired at children. (Indeed, Galloway has written for the proxy Iranian regime news propaganda site *American Herald Tribune*, which was shut down by the US Department of Justice in 2020.) Like the Soviet Israelophobic propaganda before it, this Iranian material finds an entry-point to the west via the hard-left, and from there emanates into liberal circles more generally.

This is only the tip of the iceberg. Propagandists working for Hamas, which has a strong relationship with Iran, along with other terrorist organisations, regularly spew out sophisticated Israelophobic propaganda, which as we have seen makes its way into the western mainstream via the portal of social justice. Routinely, activists take footage of violence in Syria or elsewhere and present it falsely as Israeli brutality, alongside avalanches of memes, cartoons and videos presenting false facts as the truth. As Orwell put it, 'one of the marks of antisemitism is an ability to believe stories that could not possibly be true.'[95] With the Israelophobic virus already infecting great swathes of the liberal left, this relentless propaganda effort has a receptive audience, packaged as it is in the language of anti-colonialism, anti-racism and anti-fascism. It has been hugely effective in co-opting well-meaning western liberals.

Chapter Six

THE EIGHT GIVEAWAYS AND THE FIVE PRESSURE POINTS

This book, I hope, has shown how Israelophobia is not a new phenomenon but simply the latest face of a many-headed monster. Its roots can be traced back thousands of years. The antisemitism that followed the death of Christ two thousand years ago dominated for many centuries until it was subsumed into a larger, race-based ideology exemplified by the Nazis; that in turn has become subsumed in a consuming hatred for the Jewish state. Along the way, the extensive efforts of teams of propagandists in Berlin, Moscow and Tehran have crafted the falsification with such skill that it has become a part of the way many people talk and think. In many ways, the past century has comprised a battleground to mould the modern mind, and first in the firing line have been the Jews.

But it is the old animus. It rests upon the same conspiracy theories and muttered assumptions that have been so deeply embedded in our culture for so long that they can pass without remark. Israelophobia is like a familiar language, pronounced in a new accent, or a hateful narrative written in a different font, or a remake of an unpleasant classic movie. As Jacobson put it: 'To its enemies, of course, Israel didn't disappoint expectations, it confirmed them. What else but genocide and apartheid was to be expected of a people who kept company with the devil and drank the blood of Gentile children?'[1]

Overcoming Israelophobia begins with identifying it. Since it masquerades so insistently as anti-racism or social justice, this can be tricky. Here are eight giveaways:

1. The old antisemitic conspiracy theories about Jews controlling the financial markets, media and politics are presented again, only now with Israel or the Mossad pulling the strings.
2. Soviet propaganda is regurgitated, featuring tropes like: Israel is a racist or fascist state; Zionism is colonialism; Israelis are as bad as the Nazis; Israel practises apartheid, ethnic cleansing and genocide; the Holocaust was exaggerated and is exploited to win sympathy; and diaspora Jews are a fifth column serving Israeli interests.
3. Persecution suffered by the Jewish people is rehashed and blamed on the Jews themselves; for example, accusing Israel of conducting a Holocaust on the Palestinians.
4. Israel is portrayed as the worst country on Earth and the crimes of other countries, even those that are far worse, and even those nearby in the region, are ignored.
5. Israel's flaws are used to undermine its very legitimacy rather than assigning blame to those responsible.
6. The history of the Jewish people in the land of Israel is denied.

7. Israel is accused of having 'no right to exist', based on erroneous allegations of illegality, colonialism, white supremacy and racism.
8. The Jewish state is held to moral standards that no other country upholds or has ever upheld.

That is not a comprehensive list; there are more giveaways than that, and many are quite subtle. But even once you have identified Israelophobia, taking it on can be fiendishly difficult. Because of its deep cultural purchase, even getting people to recognise it is a struggle. Those who habitually oppose the Jewish state have often encountered accusations of antisemitism already, so they will have their stock defences prepared. Chief of these – as we have seen – is the 'I'm not antisemitic, only anti-Zionist' argument; challenge this and you will inevitably be accused of trying to stifle criticism of Israel. Using the concept of Israelophobia and its tripartite definition will help, but it won't be long until the hatred morphs to evade detection and seeks a haven elsewhere. For the moment, however, there is a need for a quick and easy way to draw Israelophobia out of its carapace of rhetoric.

Try this. There are at least five pressure points that may help to prise open an Israelophobia sufferer's protective shell and expose the soft body of unexamined assumptions beneath. They can be prodded in the form of questions; you'll know you've hit the spot when your counterpart can only reach for familiar defences, even though these have already been outmanoeuvred.

Not every question will work with everyone, of course.

Those of Palestinian descent, for instance, may have a very good and reasonable answer to the first. But if you hit on the right combination in the right language at the right moment, you may be able to open up the debates explored in this book. And if you do not manage to change the mind of the person with whom you are debating – how often does that happen? – you may be able to positively influence the people in earshot, or at least to make them think.

1. *What has it got to do with you?*

From the streets of Manchester to the campuses of Michigan, many Israelophobes have no dog in the fight. With no connection to the region, they could have chosen to campaign for the rights of the Afro-Brazilians or the Torres Strait Islanders or the ethnic pygmies of central Africa who suffer at the hands of the Bantu peoples. That's not to say that focusing on one injustice is wrong in itself. (I'm not talking about reasonable campaigners here, only the ones basing their arguments on falsification and demonisation.) But why do so many plump for the Palestinians?

It is hard to argue that it is out of concern for their welfare. If that was the case, campaigners would have been equally vocal when Assad bombed the Palestinian community in Yarmouk or when Hamas has oppressed its own people; on a broader note, since incomparably more innocent Muslims are killed by Islamic terrorists and tyrants than by Israel, you'd expect them to have a thing or two to say about that.

There are usually two true explanations. First: the Palestinian cause has become an ideological totem for the leftist revolutionary instinct and a collective expression of the political identity of adherents.

Second: the Jews.

2. *Can you accept that Israel has many admirable qualities, especially when compared to the other states in the region? If not, why not?*

Reasonable critics are not threatened by Israel's praiseworthy aspects. Being free from prejudice, they see the country's liberal attitude towards same-gender relationships, for example, or its (albeit imperfect) protection of minority rights, as things to be celebrated. Israelophobia, however, rests on demonisation, which exaggerates the evils of Israel and maligns it as the world's foremost harmful force. If praise for these things sticks in a person's craw, that may suggest the existence of bigotry. For the worst sufferers, even Israel's wonderful food is hard to accept.

Needless to say, there are also many positive aspects of Palestinian society, such as its characteristic hospitality, loyalty, familial and communal solidarity and respect for elders, not to mention its cuisine. This should be easy to recognise, too.

3. *Are you able to articulate your criticism without repeating long-discredited Soviet lies and other falsifications?*

The repetition of agitprop is the real giveaway of Israelophobia, setting it aside from legitimate criticism. This includes falsified accusations of genocide, apartheid, white supremacy, settler colonialism and so on. As we have seen, each slur is easy enough to disprove but they often feel right on account of their familiarity. It is rare to find anyone who knows that this stuff was cooked up by propagandists in Moscow or Nazi Berlin.

4. *There are far worse injustices and human rights abuses all over the world, particularly in the Middle East. Right?*
From the Ukraine maelstrom to the civil wars in Yemen and Myanmar – the latter alone claimed about 20,000 lives in 2022, compared to 255 deaths in the Israel–Palestinian conflict[2] – the plight of the Palestinians is sadly dwarfed by examples of suffering and dispossession all over the world. Free from the influence of prejudice, this should be an easy enough fact to acknowledge; after all, it need not detract from sympathy for the Palestinians. However, Israelophobia, as we have seen, rests on demonisation. If that is your world-view, accepting the true scale of the conflict is hard.

5. *What country has a better moral record than Israel?*
Due to the influence of demonisation, the idea that Israel has a decent moral record seems outrageous. Compare it to Britain and the United States, for example, with their history of empire, overseas meddling, racial oppression and foreign wars, and the case becomes less clear-cut. Compare it to its neighbours and there's simply no contest. Moreover, the Jewish state faces the most intense security challenges of any democracy. Given the track record of the others – British forces in Ireland or the RAF in Dresden, the American-led invasion of Iraq – would any of them do any better? Why is Israel always held to a standard of behaviour that no country in history has ever achieved?

These questions may help. But the problem is not easily solved. Part of the challenge is that as the culture wars rage, Israel has become linked to people's political identities. When Israelophobia became the cultural default of Corbyn's Labour Party, the queue for the Conservative Friends of Israel event at Tory conference seemed to stretch for miles; when Sir Keir Starmer took over as leader of Labour, with change in the wind, the queues outside the Labour Friends of Israel event were even longer than those at the Tory one. Where does all this leave the Jews?

What we must work towards is a future in which Israel is neither demonised nor fetishised but treated for what it is: remarkable in many ways, troubling in many others, but ultimately, with its heroes and its villains, just another country. Only then will we see the end of Israelophobia.

ENDNOTE

I am not, in fact, the first person to have come up with the term 'Israelophobia'. The first thing I did when I thought of it was type it into Google. I discovered that the Italian-Israeli journalist Fiamma Nirenstein had used the term before, though without my definition and contextualisation, and it had not entered widespread circulation. As I understand it, the word was first coined in the nineties by the historian Raphael Israeli.

ACKNOWLEDGEMENTS

Especial thanks go to the historian Simon Sebag Montefiore, whose advice was generous and indispensable. Several international academics were extremely magnanimous, including the Russian scholar Izabella Tabarovsky; Dr David Motadel, Associate Professor of International History at the London School of Economics; the political scientist and historian Matthias Küntzel; Professor Meir Litvak, Chair of the Department of Middle Eastern and African History at Tel Aviv University; Professor Elhanan Yakira of Hebrew University; Professor Andrew Roberts, who advised on Churchill and Dresden; and the ever-courteous Dr Jeffrey Herf, Distinguished University Professor Emeritus at the University of Maryland. Also thank you to the lawyer and antisemitism expert Anthony Julius, and the journalists Dominic Green and Jonathan Foreman. Orlando Radice, the *Jewish Chronicle* deputy editor, and the rest of the senior staff have my gratitude for picking up the slack with alacrity when I disappeared at awkward times to write. Finally, my extra special thanks go to Roxanna, our children and the wider family for putting up with me working all hours with the myopia of a madman. It's not easy to share your life with a writer, particularly one who also happens to be a full-time newspaper editor and who powers himself by way of cycling and whisky. My eternal gratitude to you all.

NOTES

Foreword

1 https://harvardharrispoll.com/wp-content/uploads/2023/12/HHP_Dec23_KeyResults.pdf
2 https://www.thejc.com/lets-talk/jews-dont-need-the-cult-of-woke-it-doesnt-care-for-us-cp4hbujy
3 https://www.theguardian.com/world/2004/feb/03/comment
4 https://www.nytimes.com/2023/11/07/opinion/us-jewish-israel-sept-11.html
5 https://www.orwellfoundation.com/the-orwell-foundation/orwell/essays-and-other-works/antisemitism-in-britain/
6 https://www.wsj.com/articles/when-biden-met-begin-11605828020

Chapter One: The Newest Hatred

1 https://www.thejc.com/news/news/bbc-interviews-%27we-love-death%27-activist-on-tackling-jew-hate-52WPefblECTwTCZ8tswH5P
2 https://www.thejc.com/news/news/jews-make-up-less-than-1-per-cent-of-uk-population-but-a-quarter-of-all-hate-crimes-7jnjAHPKZ1cQqLFlL3olMk
3 https://www.thejc.com/news/news/antisemitism-watchdog-launches-uk-wide-stand-with-jews-campaign-5gY61OZ4xJhBLCDhoNieyH
4 https://www.theguardian.com/commentisfree/2023/apr/15/racism-in-britain-is-not-a-black-and-white-issue-it-is-far-more-complicated

5 https://www.npr.org/2023/03/23/1165737405/antisemitism-statistics-report-2022-anti-defamation-league
6 https://www.jpost.com/diaspora/antisemitism/article-729720
7 https://www.osw.waw.pl/en/publikacje/analyses/2023-03-27/germanys-strategy-to-combat-anti-semitism
8 https://www.businessinsider.com/israel-iron-dome-blocks-90-percent-rockets-hamas-gaza-2021-5?r=US&IR=T
9 https://news.un.org/en/story/2021/12/1108352
10 Dara Horn, *People Love Dead Jews*, W. W. Norton & Co, 2021, p. 10.
11 https://www.thejc.com/news/news/bbc-apologises-after-presenter-said-israeli-forces-are-happy-to-kill-children-4JDRb7IKCqCUk6Vck6w3AJ
12 https://quillette.com/2019/11/16/thorstein-veblens-theory-of-the-leisure-class-a-status-update/
13 Elizabeth Currid-Halkett, *The Sum of Small Things: A theory of the aspirational class*, Princeton University Press, 2017.
14 https://www.btselem.org/press_releases/20230108_the_occupied_territories_in_2022_largest_number_of_palestinians_killed_by_israel_in_the_west_bank_since_2004
15 Combatants: https://www.newsweek.com/ukraine-russia-elon-muks-troop-deaths-war-1779496. Civilians: https://www.ohchr.org/en/news/2022/12/ukraine-civilian-casualty-update-19-december-2022
16 https://peoplesdispatch.org/2023/01/04/over-3000-yemenis-were-killed-or-injured-in-2022-says-report/
17 https://www.spiked-online.com/2021/11/10/the-demonisation-of-israel-is-out-of-control/
18 https://nypost.com/2023/01/14/university-of-michigan-protesters-call-for-intifada-demise-of-israel/
19 Albert H. Halsey, *The Decline of Donnish Dominion: The British Academic Professions in the Twentieth Century*, Oxford University Press, 1992, chapter 11.
20 Remi Adekoya, Eric Kaufmann and Tom Simpson, *Academic Freedom in the UK: Protecting Viewpoint Diversity*, Policy Exchange, 2020.
21 https://www.cspicenter.com/p/academic-freedom-in-crisis-punishment
22 https://www.nationalaffairs.com/publications/detail/the-constitution-of-knowledge
23 https://www.cspicenter.com/p/academic-freedom-in-crisis-punishment
24 https://www.telegraph.co.uk/news/2020/07/16/harvard-professor-stephen-pinker-attacked-550-academics-tweets/

25 https://www.insidehighered.com/news/2021/08/31/fire-launches-new-database-tracking-attacks-speech
26 https://www.insidehighered.com/news/admissions/2023/05/08/jewish-student-enrollment-down-many-ivies
27 https://www.standwithus.com/post/george-washington-university-ignored-professor-s-antisemitism-says-new-civil-rights-complaint
28 Hannah Arendt, *Eichmann in Jerusalem: A Report on the Banality of Evil*, Penguin Books, 1994, p. 150.
29 John Rees, *The ABC of Socialism*, Bookmarks, 1994, p. 55.
30 https://www.thejc.com/news/news/university-student-union-officer-slammed-after-saying-i%27d-back-hamas-in-a-conflict-with-israel-542SSNfDZ1AbY8j6V4z8EL
31 https://www.jpost.com/International/Belgian-MP-tramples-Israeli-flag-at-pro-Assad-rally-315523
32 https://www.timesofisrael.com/palestinians-celebrate-jerusalem-synagogue-massacre-with-fireworks-sweets/
33 https://www.ibtimes.co.in/wanted-kill-many-not-just-one-palestinian-enters-israel-craving-jewish-genocide-rapes-856400
34 https://www.youtube.com/watch?v=6zHL2xondgE&t=698s
35 https://web.archive.org/web/20121029025033/http://www.adl.org/extremism/karta/
36 https://www.nytimes.com/2007/01/15/nyregion/15rabbi.html
37 Howard Jacobson, *Mother's Boy*, Vintage 2023, p. 267.
38 Revelation 2:9 and 3:9
39 https://www.thetimes.co.uk/article/voters-remember-what-politicians-forget-3lslok9ngon
40 https://www.theguardian.com/media/2003/may/22/theindependent.pressandpublishing
41 https://www.theguardian.com/media/2013/jan/28/murdoch-apology-sunday-times-cartoon
42 George Orwell, *Orwell and England*, Macmillan, 2021, p. 50.

Chapter Two: Israelophobia

1 https://twitter.com/guidofawkes/status/981074670635159553
2 Theodor Herzl, *Der Judenstaat*. English, Tredition Classics, 2012, p. 5.

Chapter Three: Demonisation

1 http://downloads.bbc.co.uk/rmhttp/radio4/transcripts/1961_reith5.pdf
2 https://www.mackinac.org/OvertonWindow
3 Alan Dershowitz, *The Case for Israel*, John Wiley & Sons Inc., 2003.
4 https://www.jcpa.org/phas/phas-sharansky-f04.htm
5 https://jcpa.org/mission-impossible-repairing-the-ties-between-europe-and-israel/anti-semitism-in-europe-today-comes-mostly-from-the-left/
6 https://fra.europa.eu/en/content/fra-opinions-experiences-and-perceptions-antisemitism
7 https://fra.europa.eu/en/news/2023/major-eu-survey-antisemitism-and-jewish-life-launched
8 https://obamawhitehouse.archives.gov/blog/2010/05/03/because-i-believe-you
9 https://assets.nationbuilder.com/nus/pages/108/attachments/original/1673471780/Independent_Investigation_into_Antisemitism_Report_NUS_12_January_2023.pdf?1673471780
10 https://assets.publishing.service.gov.uk/media/59786a0040f0b65dcb00000a/042-Persecution-of-Christians-in-the-Middle-East.pdf
11 Benny Morris, *1948: Righteous Victims: A history of the Zionist–Arab conflict 1881–2001*, Vintage Books, 2001, p.252–258.
12 Avi Beker, *The Forgotten Narrative: Jewish refugees from Arab countries*, Jewish Political Studies Review, Vol. 17, No. 3 / 4, Fall 2005, p.4.
13 Noah Lewin-Epstein and Yinon Cohen (18 August 2019), *'Ethnic origin and identity in the Jewish population of Israel'*, *Journal of Ethnic and Migration Studies*, 45 (11), p.2118–2137.
14 https://www.jewishvirtuallibrary.org/jewish-refugees-from-arab-countries
15 https://www.youtube.com/watch?v=35eEljsSQfc
16 https://www.jewishvirtuallibrary.org/israel-ranking-on-democracy-index
17 https://www.transparency.org/en/cpi/2022
18 https://hdr.undp.org/data-center/human-development-index#/indicies/HDI
19 https://worldpopulationreview.com/country-rankings/crime-rate-by-country
20 https://www.jns.org/israel-ranked-fifth-safest-country-for-tourists/
21 https://www.jewishvirtuallibrary.org/total-casualties-arab-israeli-conflict
22 https://www.indexoncensorship.org/indexindex/

23 https://www.timesofisrael.com/thousands-attend-funeral-of-ballet-dancer-who-was-washed-out-to-sea/
24 https://www.bbc.co.uk/news/world-middle-east-64390817
25 https://worldhappiness.report/ed/2023/world-happiness-trust-and-social-connections-in-times-of-crisis/#ranking-of-happiness-2020-2022
26 https://il.boell.org/en/2019/04/04/poll-most-israelis-have-positive-view-jewish-arab-relations
27 https://www.pcpsr.org/en/node/931
28 https://www.timesofisrael.com/israel-divided-along-tribal-lines-rivlin-warns/
29 Morris, *1948: A History of the First Arab–Israeli War*, 2008, p. 404–406.
30 Anthony Julius, *Trials of the Diaspora*, Oxford University Press, 2012, p. xv.
31 In David Barsamian and Edward Said, *Culture and Resistance: Conversations with Edward Said*, Pluto Press, 2003, p. 54, Said said: 'The town of Hebron is essentially an Arab town. There were no Jews in it before 1967.' This was untrue. As Anthony Julius notes in *Trials of the Diaspora*, Oxford University Press, 2012, p. xiv: 'For over 2,000 years, until 1936, there was a continuous and substantial Jewish presence in Hebron, mostly tolerated, always subordinate.' Said made other questionable claims about Hebron on a number of occasions.
32 https://www.haaretz.com/israel-news/2016-08-23/ty-article/.premium/arab-students-in-jerusalem-get-less-than-half-the-funding-of-jews/0000017f-f859-d887-a7ff-f8fdad430000
33 https://www.wsj.com/articles/the-huwara-riot-was-not-a-pogrom-jews-palestinians-misappropriation-mainstream-margins-russia-95b5dabb
34 https://metro.co.uk/2023/03/27/black-children-six-times-more-likely-to-be-strip-searched-by-police-18504292/
35 https://www.thetimes.co.uk/article/police-strip-searching-children-as-young-as-eight-8vnjfrocm
36 https://www.france24.com/en/france/20210913-macron-to-increase-oversight-of-police-after-brutality-and-racism-claims
37 https://www.thetimes.co.uk/article/why-many-british-jews-will-be-horrified-by-israels-new-government-rzjvpcg7h
38 https://web.archive.org/web/20080102223444/http://www.csuohio.edu/tagar/boris.htm
39 https://unwatch.org/2022-2023-unga-resolutions-on-israel-vs-rest-of-the-world/
40 https://www.fdd.org/analysis/2022/08/24/the-time-is-now-to-reform-the-un-human-rights-apparatus/

41 https://www.un.org/unispal/human-rights-council-resolutions/
42 http://www.gicj.org/images/2019/pdfs/HRC41/The-Rise-in-Hate-Speech-by-Political-Representatives-and-on-Social-Media-in-Israel.pdf
43 https://www.thejc.com/news/israel/israel-is-the-most-targeted-country-in-the-world-on-social-media-says-new-study-pAyuIfSSheLdoy7guwtRt
44 https://www.worldjewishcongress.org/en/durban-conference?item=t4izTL3hYeaTfoPCpfHQm
45 https://www.france24.com/en/20090421-un-attempts-damage-control-after-ahmadinejad-speech-
46 Danny Danon, *In the Lion's Den: Israel and the world*, Wicked Son, 2022.
47 Mark Twain, *The Innocents Abroad*, Wordsworth Editions, 2010.
48 https://www.jpost.com/international/article-743145
49 https://freedomhouse.org/countries/freedom-world/scores
50 https://www.thejc.com/news/uk/now-end-of-zionism-academic-says-bristol-jsoc-is-israel-s-pawn-1.511915
51 https://www.nytimes.com/2022/10/19/world/middleeast/palestinian-culinary-traditions.html
52 Theodor Herzl, 'A *Solution of the Jewish Question*', *Jewish Chronicle*, January 17, 1896, p. 12.
53 Simon Sebag Montefiore, *Jerusalem: The biography*, Weidenfeld & Nicolson, 2020, p. 451.
54 Manashe Harrel, '*The Jewish Presence in Jerusalem through the Ages*' and Ori Stendel '*The Arabs in Jerusalem*', in Sinai and Oestericcher, eds., *Jerusalem*, John Day, 1974
55 http://monbalagan.com/45-chronologie-israel/des-arabes-chretiens-et-ottomans/126-1899-1er-mars-lettre-de-youssouf-diya-al-khalidi-a-herzl-premiere-opposition-au-sionisme.html?highlight=WyJsZXRocmUiLCJoZXJ6bCIsImhlcnpsaWVubmVzIl0=
56 T. E. Lawrence, Malcom Brown (ed), *T. E. Lawrence in War and Peace: An anthology of the military writings of Lawrence of Arabia*, Greenhill Books, 2005, p. 106.
57 https://www.theatlantic.com/membership/archive/2017/12/when-the-british-got-jerusalem-for-christmas/548192/
58 https://archive.jewishagency.org/maps/content/35916/
59 Joseph S. Spoerl, '*Palestinians, Arabs and the Holocaust*', *Jewish Political Studies Review* Vol. 26, numbers 1–2, March 2015, p. 25.
60 Sebag Montefiore, *Jerusalem*.
61 Benny Morris, '*Vertreibung, Flucht und Schutzbedürfnis: Wie 1948 das*

Problem der palästinensischen Flüchtlinge entstand' in *FAZ*, December 29, 2001.

62 https://www.jewishvirtuallibrary.org/latest-population-statistics-for-israel

63 https://www.thetimes.co.uk/article/akub-restaurant-review-london-giles-coren-jl6j66wrg

64 Simon Sebag Montefiore, *The World*, Weidenfeld & Nicolson, 2022, p 1078.

65 Yasmin Khan, *The Great Partition: The Making of India and Pakistan*, Yale University Press, 2008; https://www.redcross.org.uk/stories/our-movement/our-history/india-partition-the-red-cross-response-to-the-refugee-crisis

66 Morris, *1948: First Arab–Israeli War*, p. 404–406.

67 https://www.jewishvirtuallibrary.org/latest-population-statistics-for-israel

68 Sunder Katwala, *How to be a Patriot: Why love of country can end our very British culture war*, HarperNorth, 2023, p. 62.

69 https://www.unhcr.org/us/about-unhcr/who-we-are/figures-glance

70 https://www.newsweek.com/palestinians-never-miss-opportunity-miss-opportunity-opinion-1531588

71 https://www.washingtonpost.com/wp-dyn/content/article/2009/07/16/AR2009071603584.html?sid=ST2009090403399

72 https://www.bbc.co.uk/news/world-asia-63554941

73 https://edition.cnn.com/2019/02/01/world/european-colonization-climate-change-trnd/index.html

74 Sebag Montefiore, *The World*.

75 https://www.churchtimes.co.uk/articles/2005/11-february/features/ash-wednesday-1945

76 https://melaniephillips.substack.com/p/the-real-story-about-that-gaza-death

77 https://www.spectator.co.uk/article/what-the-bbc-gets-wrong-about-israel/

78 Ruth Harris, *The Man on Devil's Island: Alfred Dreyfus and the affair that divided France*, Penguin, 2011.

79 Piers Paul Read, *The Dreyfus Affair: The story of the most infamous miscarriage of justice in French history*, Bloomsbury, 2012.

80 Sebag Montefiore, *The World*, p. 483.

81 David Livingstone Smith, *Less Than Human: Why we demean, enslave and exterminate others*, Macmillan, 2011, p. 137.

82 Richard Taylor, *Film Propaganda: Soviet Russia and Nazi Germany*, IB Tauris & Co Ltd, 2009, p. 179.

83 https://jcpa.org/article/parallels-between-nazi-and-islamist-anti-semitism/
84 https://www.theatlantic.com/magazine/archive/2008/03/the-2-000-year-old-panic/306640/
85 HH Ben-Sasson (ed), *A History of the Jewish People*, Harvard University Press, 1976, p. 875.
86 https://collections.ushmm.org/search/catalog/irn2910
87 https://www.theguardian.com/world/2006/jul/31/arts.usa
88 https://encyclopedia.ushmm.org/content/en/timeline-event/holocaust/1939-1941/hitler-speech-to-german-parliament
89 Peter Longerich, *Hitler: A biography*, Oxford University Press, 2019, p. 779.
90 https://www.jewishvirtuallibrary.org/muslim-clerics-jews-are-the-descendants-of-apes-pigs-and-other-animals
91 https://www.thejc.com/news/uk-news/chris-williamson-hits-out-after-losing-his-seat-saying-foreign-government-mobilised-against-corby-1.494422
92 https://www.thejc.com/lets-talk/all/the-problem-with-miller-1.512511
93 https://www.thejc.com/news/uk/david-miller-sacked-by-bristol-1.521060
94 https://securingdemocracy.gmfus.org/british-commentators-iran-russia-ukraine-conspiracy-theories/
95 https://www.opensecrets.org/fara
96 https://www.adl.org/resources/blog/antisemitic-conspiracy-theories-abound-around-russian-assault-ukraine

Chapter Four: Weaponisation

1 Istvan Pal Adam, *Post-Holocaust Pogroms in Hungary and Poland*, Central European University, 2009, p. 1.
2 David Hirsh, *Contemporary Left Antisemitism*, Routledge, 2017, p. 5.
3 https://twitter.com/jeremycorbyn/status/824708732504473601
4 https://www.timesofisrael.com/corbyn-called-for-uks-holocaust-memorial-day-to-be-renamed/
5 https://www.independent.co.uk/news/uk/politics/labour-antisemitism-row-jeremy-corbyn-holocaust-israel-nazis-party-definition-a8472276.html
6 https://www.theguardian.com/politics/2016/jul/04/jeremy-corbyn-says-he-regrets-calling-hamas-and-hezbollah-friends

7 *'La plus belle des ruses du diable est de vous persuader qu'il n'existe pas!'* Charles Baudelaire, *The Flowers of Evil and the Generous Gambler*, Benediction Classics, 2012, p. 253.

8 https://www.bbc.co.uk/news/topics/c28q43x9qmzt

9 https://www.memri.org/tv/british-bishop-denies-holocaust-iran-tv-no-many-good-jews

10 https://www.theguardian.com/us-news/2017/aug/16/charlottesville-neo-nazis-vice-news-hbo

11 Bari Weiss, *How to Fight Anti-Semitism*, Allen Lane, 2019, p. 85.

12 https://twitter.com/jeremycorbyn/status/1194197042534461440?lang=en

13 George Spater, William Cobbett: *The Poor Man's Friend*, Cambridge University Press, 1982.

14 William Cobbett, *Political Register*, 25 October 1823, cols 214–218.

15 Cobbett, *Political Register*, 25 October 1823, col. 214–218.

16 Cobbett, *Political Register*, 5 June 1830, col. 728–735.

17 Cobbett, *Political Register*, 20 April 1805, col. 597–598.

18 Cobbett, *Political Register*, 1 March 1823, col. 565.

19 John W. Osborne, *'William Cobbett's Anti-Semitism'*, *The Historian*, Volume 47, 1984, Issue 1.

20 https://www.amnesty.org/en/location/middle-east-and-north-africa/palestine-state-of/report-palestine-state-of/

21 https://twitter.com/habibi_uk/status/1624005478916276224?lang=en

22 https://www.palestinecampaign.org/trade-unions-uk/

23 https://www.jewishnews.co.uk/spains-new-deputy-pm-called-israel-an-illegal-state/

24 https://inews.co.uk/news/politics/jeremy-corbyn-nick-griffin-bnp-support-zionists-comments-row-190234

25 Golda Meir, *My Life*, Dell Publishing Company, 1975, p. 308–309.

26 https://www.spectator.co.uk/article/blm-should-look-to-martin-luther-king-not-malcolm-x-for-inspiration/

27 Malcolm X, *The Autobiography of Malcolm X*, Penguin, 2001.

28 Patricia Bidol-Padva, *Developing New Perspectives on Race*, New Detroit, 1970.

29 https://www.theguardian.com/culture/2022/feb/02/whoopi-goldberg-suspended-from-the-view-after-saying-holocaust-isnt-about-race

30 https://www.hepi.ac.uk/2017/12/18/two-thirds-68-students-now-back-labour-think-labour-55-jeremy-corbyn-58-back-remain/

31 https://www.theguardian.com/politics/2017/oct/07/oh-jeremy-corbyn-chant-white-stripes

32 https://nymag.com/intelligencer/2020/02/this-one-chart-explains-why-young-voters-back-bernie-sanders.html
33 https://www.commentary.org/noah-rothman/bernie-sanders-has-a-big-jeremy-corbyn-problem/
34 https://www.usnews.com/news/elections/articles/2019-12-19/sanders-calls-netanyahu-racist-escalating-attacks-on-the-embattled-israeli-pm?context=amp
35 https://www.dailymail.co.uk/news/article-7742535/Jeremy-Corbyn-played-role-useful-idiot-Kremlin-undermining-Nato.html
36 https://www.dailymail.co.uk/news/article-11388081/Ukraine-brands-Jeremy-Corbyn-one-Putins-useful-idiots-hes-set-speak-propaganda-event.html
37 https://www.thearticle.com/jeremy-corbyns-shameful-links-to-irans-theocratic-tyranny
38 https://www.syriahr.com/en/291981/
39 https://www.ohchr.org/en/stories/2023/05/behind-data-recording-civilian-casualties-syria
40 https://www.jewishvirtuallibrary.org/total-casualties-arab-israeli-conflict
41 https://www.thejc.com/news/news/bbc-broadcasts-folksongs-that-glorify-attacks-on-jews-6wJhXGiv3rhgfazyMN9cAS
42 https://theweek.com/articles/488741/conspiracy-alert-egypts-sharkattack-crisis-work-israel
43 https://www.thejc.com/news/news/fury-of-local-residents-as-palestinian-flag-flies-over-lancashire-town-hall-in-jubilee-week-6VoCU7VuaZkyCIeuuiwax9
44 https://www.theguardian.com/news/2019/may/01/jeremy-corbyn-rejects-antisemitism-claim-over-book-foreword
45 https://www.thejc.com/lets-talk/all/is-it-time-for-jews-to-do-less-yearning-and-more-living-6O93osYNNU1pl8P6Cjy2qA
46 https://www.thejc.com/news/news/kate-winslet-gaza-film-%27is-hamas-propaganda%27-4HTFOwxQYtJTATLDuO8zOb
47 https://www.thejc.com/news/news/kate-winslet-gaza-film-%27is-hamas-propaganda%27-4HTFOwxQYtJTATLDuO8zOb
48 https://www.spectator.co.uk/article/the-new-york-times-revealing-gaza-coverage/
49 https://www.theguardian.com/media/2002/may/06/mondaymediasection5
50 https://www.france24.com/en/tv-shows/truth-or-fake/20211104-pallywood-truth-and-falsehoods-amid-political-communications

51 https://www.reuters.com/article/factcheck-fake-gaza-idUSL2N2N52AF
52 https://www.thejc.com/news/world/bella-hadid-slammed-for-anti-israel-posts-in-wake-of-synagogue-terror-attack-7At8BfuTnl9X7eaFauyECN
53 https://www.timesofisrael.com/israel-raps-bbc-for-unethical-terror-attack-headline/
54 https://www.theguardian.com/sport/2017/sep/24/israel-giro-ditalia-race-conflict-2018-start-cycling
55 https://www.trtworld.com/magazine/israel-s-greenwashing-weaponising-environmentalism-on-palestinian-lands-54041
56 https://www.newarab.com/analysis/israel-uses-animal-rights-vegan-wash-occupation
57 https://bdsmovement.net/pinkwashing
58 https://decolonizepalestine.com/rainbow-washing/purplewashing/
59 https://www.aljazeera.com/opinions/2022/4/9/wine-washing-the-israeli-occupation
60 Jean-Paul Sartre, *Anti-Semite and Jew*, Schocken, 1995, p. 33.
61 https://www.algemeiner.com/2023/01/06/hamas-official-interviewed-on-german-public-tv-in-latest-antisemitic-scandal/
62 Menachem Begin, *The Revolt*, Dell, 1977, p. 313.
63 Noah Lewin-Epstein and Yinon Cohen, ibid., p. 2118–2137.
64 https://antisemitism.org/jews-over-five-times-more-likely-to-be-targets-of-hate-crimes-than-other-faith-group-caa-analysis-of-home-office-stats-shows/
65 https://forward.com/news/415385/is-a-string-of-attacks-against-brooklyn-jews-really-about-anti-semitism/
66 https://www.jstor.org/stable/43822935
67 https://www.spectator.co.uk/article/does-israel-train-america-s-police-forces/
68 https://www.jta.org/2020/06/02/united-states/los-angeles-jews-take-stock-after-george-floyd-protests-batter-local-institutions/
69 https://www.timesofisrael.com/protesters-shout-dirty-jews-at-paris-rally-against-police-racism/
70 David Baddiel called it 'Schrodinger's whites'. David Baddiel, *Jews Don't Count*, TLS, 2021, p. 73.
71 https://www.orwellfoundation.com/the-orwell-foundation/orwell/essays-and-other-works/antisemitism-in-britain/
72 https://web.archive.org/web/20080102223444/http://www.csuohio.edu/tagar/boris.htm

73 https://www.ngo-monitor.org/fact-sheet-ken-roth/
74 https://www.channel4.com/programmes/david-baddiel-jews-dont-count
75 Baddiel, *Jews Don't Count*, p. 90–93.
76 https://twitter.com/baddiel/status/1205468962345177088?lang=eu
77 Baddiel, *Jews Don't Count*, p. 90.
78 Baddiel, *Jews Don't Count*, p. 91.
79 Baddiel, *Jews Don't Count*, p. 92.
80 Dennis Ross, *The Missing Peace: The Inside Story of the Fight for Middle East Peace*, Farrar, Straus and Giroux, 2005, p. 694.
81 https://www.wayoflife.org/reports/temple_denial_vs_archaeology.html
82 https://content.time.com/time/subscriber/article/0,33009,493263,00.html
83 Dore Gold, *The Fight for Jerusalem: Radical Islam, the West and the Future of the Holy City*, Regnery Publishing, 2007.
84 https://www.theguardian.com/world/2016/oct/14/israel-unesco-resolution-jerusalem-palestine
85 https://web.archive.org/web/20080102223444/http://www.csuohio.edu/tagar/boris.htm
86 Herzl, 'A *Solution*', p. 12.
87 https://www.thejc.com/news/news/bbc-apologises-after-presenter-said-israeli-forces-are-happy-to-kill-children-4JDRb7IKCqCUk6Vck6w3AJ
88 https://www.thejc.com/lets-talk/all/jews-in-their-own-words-so-long-as-they-don%27t-say-%27israel%27-6tRo9LjpbgX4XQrdvBgJwk
89 Arendt, *Eichmann in Jerusalem*, p. 85.
90 https://www.dailymail.co.uk/columnists/article-11874055/ANDREW-NEIL-easy-scoff-woke-nonsense-like-Oxfams-language-guide-not-fad.html
91 https://yougov.co.uk/topics/politics/articles-reports/2021/12/22/cancel-culture-what-views-are-britons-afraid-expre
92 John Milton, *Areopagitica and Other Writings*, Penguin, 2014.
93 https://www.britainschoice.co.uk/
94 https://www.the-tls.co.uk/articles/problem-hyper-liberalism-essay-john-gray/
95 https://www.kcl.ac.uk/news/uk-culture-war-debate-public-divide-into-four-groups-not-two-warring-tribes
96 https://www.jta.org/2017/06/25/united-states/marchers-carrying-jewish-pride-flags-asked-to-leave-chicago-dyke-march
97 https://www.change.org/p/lesbians-attacked-at-san-francisco-dyke-march-demand-retraction-of-libelous-statements

98 https://www.feministcurrent.com/2018/08/13/lesbians-excluded-vancouver-dyke-march-name-inclusivity/
99 https://www.thejc.com/lets-talk/all/like-corbynism-the-gender-debate-has-gone-through-the-looking-glass-1L9eUHjLSVsgO2b52uRIph
100 https://www.amnesty.org/en/latest/news/2022/02/israels-apartheid-against-palestinians-a-cruel-system-of-domination-and-a-crime-against-humanity/
101 Trevor Noah, *Born a Crime: Stories from a South African childhood*, John Murray, 2017.
102 https://www.timesofisrael.com/khaled-kabub-sworn-in-as-supreme-courts-first-muslim-justice/
103 https://www.tandfonline.com/doi/abs/10.1080/17511321.2020.1770848?journalCode=rsep20
104 https://twitter.com/YosephHaddad/status/1639728828900581377?s=20
105 https://www.jpost.com/arab-israeli-conflict/palestinian-authority-youre-a-traitor-if-you-sell-land-to-the-jews-619368
106 https://www.washingtoninstitute.org/policy-analysis/israels-security-fence-effective-reducing-suicide-attacks-northern-west-bank
107 https://thespectator.com/topic/has-micah-goodman-found-the-path-to-peace/
108 *'The Arab Boycott and Apartheid'*, *Arab Outlook* 1/2, December 1963, in Dave Rich, *The Left's Jewish Problem*, Biteback, 2018, p. 38.
109 https://www.ohchr.org/sites/default/files/Documents/Issues/Truth/CallLegacyColonialism/CSO/Al-Haq-Annex-3.pdf
110 Sartre, *Anti-Semite and Jew*, p. 13.
111 https://www.timesofisrael.com/amnestys-israel-chief-criticizes-groups-report-accusing-israel-of-apartheid/
112 https://www.thejc.com/news/news/revealed-amnesty%27s-own-officials-reject-%27apartheid%27-smear-1Hgn4ETJJkQk9a7iSASNCv
113 Rich, *Left's Jewish Problem*, p. 36.
114 https://assets.nationbuilder.com/nus/pages/108/attachments/original/1673471780/Independent_Investigation_into_Antisemitism_Report_NUS_12_January_2023.pdf?1673471780

Chapter Five: Falsification

1 Edward Horne, *A Job Well Done: A history of the Palestine police force 1920–1948*, Book Guild Publishing, 2003.

2 David Motadel, *Islam and Nazi Germany's War*, Harvard University Press, 2014, p. 39.
3 Yuval Arnon-Ohanna, *The Internal Struggle Within the Palestinian National Movement* 1929–1939, Shiloah Center, 1981, p.286, puts the number of Arabs killed by other Arabs at 4,500, based on a Palestinian source, while the Encyclopaedia Britannica estimates the entire number of Arabs killed in the Revolt at 5,000: https://www.britannica.com/place/Palestine/The-Arab-Revolt
4 Stefan Wild, '*"Mein Kampf" in arabischer Übersetzung*', *Die Welt des Islams* 9, 1–4, 1964, p. 207–211.
5 Spoerl, *'Palestinians, Arabs'*, p.15.
6 Spoerl, *'Palestinians, Arabs'*, p.16.
7 Jeffrey Herf, *Nazi Propaganda for the Arab World*, Yale University Press, 2009, p.ix-xvii.
8 Spoerl, *'Palestinians, Arabs'*, p.18.
9 Herf, *Nazi Propaganda*, p. 92.
10 Abd al-Karim al-Umar ed., *Mudhakkirat al-Hajj Muhammad Amin al -Husayni (The Memoirs of Hajj Muhammad Amin al-Husseini)*, Damascus, 1999, p. 108.
11 Motadel, *Islam and Nazi Germany's War*, p. 63.
12 Sebag Montefiore, *Jerusalem*, p. 546–547.
13 Motadel, *Islam and Nazi Germany's War*, p. 43.
14 Sebag Montefiore, *Jerusalem*, p. 547.
15 Sebag Montefiore, *Jerusalem*, p. 547.
16 Spoerl, *'Palestinians, Arabs'*, p.22.
17 https://www.tabletmag.com/sections/news/articles/amin-al-husseini-nazi-concentration-camp
18 Klaus Gensicke, *The Mufti of Jerusalem and the Nazis*, Vallentine Mitchell & Co, 2015, p.122.
19 Gilbert Achcar, *The Arabs and the Holocaust: The Arab–Israeli war of narratives*, Saqi Books, 2011.
20 https://www.jpost.com/israel-news/never-before-seen-document-penned-by-nazi-leader-himmler-uncovered-by-national-library-485539
21 Message to German foreign minister Joachim von Ribbentrop, quoted in Klaus Gensicke, *Der Mufti von Jerusalem, Amin el-Husseini, und die Nationalsozialisten*, Peter Lang, 1988.
22 Barry Rubin and Wolfgang Schwanitz, *Nazis, Islamists, and the Making of the Modern Middle East*, Yale University Press 2014, p.163.

23 Gensicke, *Der Mufti von Jerusalem.*
24 Information Sheet on Yunis Bahri, n.d. (July 1939), sent by Lampson (Embassy Cairo) to Halifax (Foreign Office), 6 July 1939, Alexandria, NA, FO 395/664, quoted in Motadel, ibid., p. 93.
25 Herf, *Nazi Propaganda*, p. 198.
26 Gensicke, *Der Mufti von Jerusalem.*
27 Herf, *Nazi Propaganda*, p. 101–102.
28 Herf, *Nazi Propaganda*, p. 105
29 Herf, *Nazi Propaganda*, p. 105–106.
30 https://nymag.com/intelligencer/article/marjorie-taylor-greene-qanon-wildfires-space-laser-rothschild-execute.html
31 Herf, *Nazi Propaganda*, p. 126.
32 Herf, *Nazi Propaganda*, p. 237.
33 https://www.tabletmag.com/sections/history/articles/the-nazi-roots-of-islamist-hate
34 Bernard Lewis, *Semites and Anti-Semites: An inquiry into conflict and prejudice*, W. W. Norton & Co 1999, p. 160.
35 Zvi Elpeleg, *Through the Eyes of the Mufti: The essays of Haj Amin*, Vallentine Mitchell & Co, 2009, p. 26.
36 Herf, *Nazi Propaganda.*
37 Zvi Elpeleg, *The Grand Mufti: Haj Amin al-Hussaini, Founder of the Palestinian National Movement*, Routledge 1993, p. 115, 120, 124–128.
38 Spoerl, '*Palestinians, Arabs*', p. 24.
39 Paul Berman, *Terror and Liberalism*, W. W. Norton and Company, 2003.
40 Matthias Küntzel, *Djihad und Judenhaß: Über den neuen antijüdischen Krie*, Ca Ira, 2002.
41 https://embassies.gov.il/holysee/AboutIsrael/the-middle-east/Pages/The%20Hamas-Covenant.aspx
42 Matthias Küntzel, *Jihad and Jew-Hatred: Islamism, Nazism and the roots of 9/11*, Telos Press Publishing, 2007, p. xxi.
43 Christian Eggers, '*Die Juden warden brennen – Die antisemitischen Wahnvorstellungen der Hamburger Al Qaida-Zelle um Mohammed Atta*', in Matthias Küntzel, *Heimliches Einverständnis? Islamischer antisemitismus und deutsche politic*, LIT-publisher, 2007.
44 https://www.tabletmag.com/sections/history/articles/the-nazi-roots-of-islamist-hate
45 Gensike, *The Mufti of Jerusalem*, p. 182–183.
46 Gensike, *The Mufti of Jerusalem*, p. 182–183.

47 Benny Morris, *The Birth of the Palestinian Refugee Problem Revisited*, Cambridge Universty Press 2004, p.23.
48 Nicholas Bethell, *The Palestinian Triangle: The struggle between the British, the Jews and the Arabs* 1935-48, Andre Deutsch, London 1979, p. 349.
49 Morris, *The Birth of the Palestinian*, p. 408–409.
50 Küntzel, *Jihad and Jew-Hatred*, p. 51.
51 https://archive.jewishagency.org/maps/content/35916/
52 Spoerl, *'Palestinians, Arabs'*, p. 15.
53 https://www.tabletmag.com/sections/history/articles/the-nazi-roots-of-islamist-hate
54 https://www.memri.org/reports/saudi-columnist-condemns-sympathy-hitler-arab-world
55 https://observer.com/2002/06/can-wieseltier-dcs-big-mullah-have-it-both-ways/
56 https://www.nytimes.com/2002/10/26/world/anti-semitic-elders-of-zion-gets-new-life-on-egypt-tv.html
57 https://www.israelhayom.com/2023/01/05/palestinian-village-elder-claims-israel-trained-cattle-for-espionage/
58 https://www.israelnationalnews.com/news/208696
59 https://www.adl.org/sites/default/files/Press-Conference-Deck-v4-May-12-2014.pdf
60 https://twitter.com/HonestReporting/status/1624746548675354624
61 https://www.memri.org/tv/uae-islamic-scholar-waseem-yousef-arabs-responsible-sectarian-war-division-in-the-region
62 https://www.institute.global/insights/geopolitics-and-security/think-again-inside-modernisation-new-middle-east
63 https://www.tabletmag.com/sections/history/articles/the-nazi-roots-of-islamist-hate
64 https://fathomjournal.org/balfour-100-chaim-weizmann-the-guardian-and-the-balfour-declaration/
65 https://fathomjournal.org/balfour-100-before-balfour-the-labour-partys -war-aims-memorandum/#_ftn2
66 Susie Linfield, *The Lion's Den: Zionism and the Left from Hannah Arendt to Noam Chomsky*, Yale University Press, 2019.
67 https://www.jstor.org/stable/26554993
68 Ion Mihai Pacepa, Professor Ronald J. Rychlak, *Disinformation: Former spy chief reveals secret strategies for undermining freedom, attacking religion, and promoting terrorism*, WND Books, 2013, p. 99.

69 https://www.washingtonpost.com/archive/politics/1979/07/15/soviet-jews-see-growth-in-anti-semitismsoviet-jews-are-fearful-of-rising-anti-semitism/9d822731-c7cc-4d1f-9af7-7fb13827410d/
70 Izabella Tabarovsky, *Demonisation Blueprints: Soviet Conspiracist Antizionism in Contemporary Left-Wing Discourse*', *Journal of Contemporary Antisemitism*, vol. 5, 2022, p. 7.
71 Tabarovsky, '*Demonisation Blueprints*', p. 3.
72 https://www.scribd.com/doc/115762049/Caution-Zionism-Yuri-Ivanov-1970
73 http://collections.americanjewisharchives.org/ms/ms0603/ms0603.072.004.pdf
74 https://www.theguardian.com/politics/2023/feb/01/labour-mp-apologises-to-commons-after-calling-israeli-government-fascist
75 https://www.telegraph.co.uk/politics/2023/02/18/labour-candidate-called-israel-apartheid-state/
76 https://fathomjournal.org/soviet-anti-zionism-and-contemporary-left-antisemitism/
77 Pacepa, *Disinformation*.
78 Pacepa, *Disinformation*.
79 https://www.tabletmag.com/sections/arts-letters/articles/mahmoud-abbas-soviet-dissertation
80 https://www.commentary.org/articles/daniel-moynihan/the-politics-of-human-rights/
81 George Orwell, *Orwell and England*, Macmillan, 2021, p. 50.
82 Baruch A Hazan, *Soviet Propaganda: A Case Study of the Middle East Conflict*, Routledge, 2017, p. 150.
83 Robert Wistrich, *From Ambivalence to Betrayal: the Left, the Jews, and Israel*, University of Nebraska Press, 2012.
84 https://www.dailymail.co.uk/news/article-6738195/CORBYN.html
85 https://www.timesofisrael.com/uks-labour-suspends-another-member-over-comments-against-jews/
86 Tabarovsky, '*Demonisation Blueprints*', p. 8.
87 Tabarovsky, '*Demonisation Blueprints*', p. 12.
88 https://www.cpusa.org/party_voices/convention-discussion-zionism-is-a-form-of-racism/
89 Tabarovsky, '*Demonisation Blueprints*', p. 15.
90 https://newleftreview.org/issues/i43/articles/che-guevara-vietnam-must-not-stand-alone
91 https://fathomjournal.org/soviet-anti-zionism-and-contemporary-left-antisemitism/

92 Jovan Byford, *Conspiracy Theories: A critical introduction*, Palgrave Macmillan, 2011, p. 62.
93 https://www.jstor.org/stable/20101082
94 https://www.thejc.com/news/world/exclusive-iran%27s-shadowy-uk-network-revealed-1.517965
95 https://www.orwellfoundation.com/the-orwell-foundation/orwell/essays-and-other-works/antisemitism-in-britain/

Chapter Six: The Eight Giveaways and the Five Pressure Points

1 https://www.thejc.com/lets-talk/all/is-it-time-for-jews-to-do-less-yearning-and-more-living-6O93osYNNU1pl8P6Cjy2qA
2 https://acleddata.com/dashboard/#/dashboard